FROM HENDON TO PENSION

FROM HENDON
TO PENSION

A Life in the Met

Clive Smith

Book Guild Publishing

Sussex, England

First published in Great Britain in 2010 by
The Book Guild Ltd
Pavilion View
19 New Road
Brighton, BN1 1UF

Typesetting in Garamond by
SetSystems Ltd, Saffron Walden, Essex

Printed in Great Britain by
CPI Antony Rowe

A catalogue record for this book is available from
the British Library

ISBN 978 1 84624 501 5

For my wife
Yvonne
and our three children

Contents

Preface

I joined the Metropolitan Police Service (MPS), often known simply as 'the Met' in the late 1970s and during my thirty years' service there were a large number of changes. Much debate invariably took place in a police canteen over the rights and, invariably, far more wrongs of each and every one of those changes.

Two weeks before I retired, I sat in a London coffee shop with two of my colleagues, who asked me what I was going to do. In truth I had little idea and the few ideas that I did have were sketchy at best, with no real plan attached. During our expensive cappuccino, one of them spoke of a book his brother had planned to write and how everyone had at least one good idea and potential for a book. This is mine.

The conversation then led to me discussing some of the funny events I had been involved in and even more that I had heard about over early morning cups of tea as the stories were slightly embellished to make them sound more interesting to the listener. Certainly when I was a young constable there were plenty of good story-tellers.

Just a day before my retirement I was back in the very nice coffee shop with my wife and sister-in-law. We were visiting London for afternoon tea later that day at a posh hotel and I also had to drop my warrant card in to my station. For thirty years my warrant card had travelled with me. Did I feel any different, they both asked me? No not just yet, there were no obvious signs of changes. I wasn't reverting back to the young lad who joined, although I wouldn't have minded the full head of hair again and a bit less grey perhaps, even a slimmer waistline.

Of course the inevitable conversation came around to what was I going to do post the Met. I mentioned the subject of the book again and as I did this my sister-in-law pointed to one of the famous blue plaques you find in London depicting some historic fact. This one was about Charles Dickens, and was positioned high on a wall opposite us. 'There you go, he wasn't too bad a writer, but don't get ideas of grandeur. Perhaps you should go for *A Christmas Cracker* instead of *A Christmas Carol*.'

These conversations led me to mention the book over a family meal. I also reflected on my thirty years of police service and was grateful for the fact that I had spent most of my working life doing something that I enjoyed. It had been a great job and a wonderful experience – and even the bad experiences had provided a positive approach to something else later in life.

My children encouraged me further to write this book, which concentrates on some of those stories I am able to tell, which provide an insight into the life of an average copper. Due to the nature of the job, when I returned home and was asked by my children what it was like to be a policeman, I concentrated on the funny side rather than the dark side, which accompanies it. I presume that is why two of my children are also serving officers and just two days after retiring I accompanied my daughter to Hendon.

My wife has never been able to see anything wrong in what I have done, always encouraging me, even having to put up with me for the last near-on twenty-seven years, along with all the pressures that policing can bring. I doubt I could have managed at times without knowing she was there.

Without doubt the family members of police officers live and sleep the job as much as the officers themselves in many ways. I am proud to have served as a police officer, but unfortunately all too often there is only negative press, which is undeserved as far more good is done by officers than bad.

List of Abbreviations

ABS anti-locking braking system.

area car the big fast cars used at the stations to respond to 999 calls. Sometimes known as the R/T car.

BIU Borough Intelligence Unit.

CO19 currently known as SO19, this is the Met's firearms command.

CPR cardiopulmonary resuscitation.

CCTV closed circuit television.

charge room later known as the custody suite, where the prisoners are taken; includes the cells.

collator later became the BIU – Borough Intelligence Unit.

custody officer sergeant in charge of the custody suit/charge room.

DPG Diplomatic Protection Group. This department protects Downing Street and a number of embassies as well as providing an armed response in Central London.

divisional surgeon later became known as the FME – forensic medical examiner. A doctor who attends the police station to examine officers, witnesses or prisoners.

duty officer the inspector in charge of a police relief for each shift.

EBM evidential breath machine.

FART first aid refresher training.

form 54 used to place a police vehicle in need of repair.

form 163 details of a complaint made against a police officer.

form 611 personal details of a defendant, their family and earnings. Completed before a court appearance.

form 728 used by officers for general reports or requests.

GBH grievous bodily harm. A very serious assault.

green goddess coach used to transport officers when they were on aid at football matches or marches.

HORT/1 this is a form a police officer issues to drivers for them to produce their driving documents.

India 99 call sign for the MPS helicopter.

IR information room.

JP Justice of the Peace.

MDT mobile data terminal. Effectively allows officers to receive calls and conduct checks from their patrol cars.

MPS Metropolitan Police Service, or simply known as the Met.

MPU Marine Police Unit.

NSPIS National Strategy for Police Information. This in English means it is an electronic machine for taking fingerprints.

NSY New Scotland Yard, the headquarters of the Metropolitan Police, based at Broadway, London, SW1.

PACE Police and Criminal Evidence Act.

POLACC police accident: a police car either involved in, or at the vicinity of, an accident.

POLCOL this replaced the above term, and means police collision.

PDRs Performance Development Reviews, better known as appraisals. Completed on an annual basis for all police officers after completion of their two-year probationary period.

PNC Police National Computer. Enables officers to perform vehicle and name checks.

RSPCA Royal Society for the Protection of Cruelty to Animals.

R/T radio transmitter. This was simply a radio that was originally fitted into only a few police vehicles, e.g. the area car, and was known as the 'R/T set'.

RVP rendezvous point.

skipper/sarge commonly used names for a sergeant.

teleprinter messages could be sent and received on a teleprinter before the age of the computer.

TSG Territorial Support Group. This department deals with major public order situations and serious disorder.

1

Training School

The Metropolitan Police training school is based at Hendon in North London. It is a huge estate and in the 1970s it housed the detective training school, as well as the recruit training school, the driving school, plus the skidpan. To say that it was a daunting experience for a young man, for me was something of an understatement. I had been on one foreign holiday and in truth knew little of the real world; all of that was soon to change.

I had been accepted in to the Metropolitan Police Force, now known as a 'Service', at my second attempt. My first attempt failed at the medical, due to a common enough problem faced by youngsters – acne. To make matters worse on that particular day I had an outbreak that could have won Olympic medals. Undeterred I applied a year later and successfully navigated myself through the entrance exam, touching my toes whilst a doctor sat five yards away, casting an experienced eye over my butt. Should you ever be faced with a similar situation ensure that your paperwork is up to scratch! At the interview I was asked a variety of questions by the board, all of whom were senior officers.

'You seem to talk quietly,' one of the officers said. 'How will you cope on the street?'

'Well sir, as a cashier I keep my voice down so that other people can't overhear someone else's business, but I believe I would adapt myself according to the circumstances.'

Weeks later a letter arrived confirming that I would be offered a place in the Met, with further details to follow after they had conducted a number of background checks on me and my family. My days in banking were finally numbered. It was several months later when I received a start date and I began training in earnest, running every evening and swimming whenever possible in preparation for the gruelling weeks that I anticipated were ahead.

It was with some relief that I handed my notice in to the bank, which I was certainly not cut out for. A few of my relatives asked me if I was doing the right thing – after all, I had a job for life, cheap loans and cheap mortgages available in later years. I wasn't having any of it though, my mind was made up.

Finally the day arrived and I delivered myself with my 1.6 white Capri to the security guard with my introductory letter and was swiftly guided to where I had to park and report. The walk from the car park to the tower block seemed to make that lonely and lost feeling in the pit of my stomach even worse as I humped my suitcase containing all the necessary kit that I could anticipate to need in the coming weeks. At one of the three residential blocks, which can be seen from the Northern Line, I was directed to my new home for the next three months, which if successful would see recruits complete three stages of training before being delivered as probationary constables to their new stations.

Perhaps if we had the mobile phone then I could have spoken to one of my brothers, or my parents, and discussed how I was feeling. I did let my mum know I had arrived safely and as always in her true parenting style she wished me good luck and told me I could only ever do my best, something she had done on every important occasion during my school years. It left me with a lump in my throat for no good reason, possibly because I was going to miss the family Sunday tea, and instead sit in a room with a bed, a wardrobe and a sink, with a view of an empty sports field and a parade ground.

2

Sworn in and Sworn at

The next morning I, along with my new class colleagues, was given the rules of the establishment and finally I was given my warrant number after swearing to carry out my duties as a constable. Despite feeling like going home and back to my job in banking I knew that this was the job I wanted to do, helping those at a time when they would most need a hand. Unlike the modern recruit, we were not entrusted with a warrant card at this stage; that would be handed to those recruits who successfully navigated their way through numerous tests, before being thrown upon the general public.

Our class, of approximately thirty and predominantly blokes, was introduced to our instructor for the next five weeks. Each recruit had a lanyard, which depicted their particular stage of training, the junior being red. Later this would be replaced with yellow (intermediate) and finally the senior band, which was red and yellow. After completing the administration, we found ourselves being measured for our uniforms and taken off to class.

At that time the Met provided you with old-fashioned schooling, with all of you sitting in a classroom, facing front and listening. At the end of the day you would be given reports to learn 'word perfect'. It was like going back to primary school, when you learned your times tables. I, along with many others, found this very hard and it took me some time before I settled into a routine. I rarely left my room apart from meal times and did not stray to the on-site bar, choosing to concentrate on my studies and ensure that each evening my trousers and tunic were pressed. Failure to maintain a satisfactory dress code could result in a punishment, which included walking the estate for an hour and ensuring that any rubbish was picked up. Not that there would be much of that and if so certainly not dropped by a recruit; more likely from some crusty old copper on their detective training course.

After a few weekends of returning to friends and family on a Friday night I fell into a routine, although I never totally adjusted to pulling up at the gates of Hendon for another week, late on a Sunday evening; but I just got on with it. Each morning consisted of a parade, when at 8 a.m. a roll call would take place, with a drill sergeant and a senior officer in attendance.

Drill sergeants were definitely a breed of their own. The police are far from a military establishment, but the drill staff were always immaculate, far more so than most recruits could ever hope to be, which allowed them to comment on the poor state you were in.

In my class we had a few ex-cadets. Cadets joined at the age of 16 before being allowed to go to Hendon at 18. They had spent a large amount of their time getting fit and learning some of the ropes that would assist them in their early weeks. Unfortunately, the Met decided to end this, which I think was a great shame.

On one particular occasion the drill sergeant, who had a fearsome reputation, took us for drill. Although we were taught to march, you would never do it again, unless you were unfortunate enough to be involved in a Force funeral. Our drill sergeant declared that his name was Butcher: 'Butcher by name and Butcher by nature!' Of course much of this was bravado. On this occasion he stood square on to an ex-cadet and poked him in the chest with his swagger stick, shouting (it was always a shout), 'I seem to have a piece of shit at the end of my stick!'

The PC quickly replied, 'Well it's not at my end sergeant.'

Twenty-nine other recruits swallowed a guffaw as the drill sergeant exploded, marching the PC away to what we feared at that time would be some painful experience. He was given a week of rubbish collection and a verbal tirade that would be replayed over the coming weeks, until someone else fell foul of an instructor.

Before we were allowed to have a police uniform our drill sergeant explained the need for each constable to have two pairs of serviceable shoes and/or boots. It was our good fortune that he just so happened to have a good supplier of boots, which of course required a good price. Most of us being unaware of this rule and not wishing to fall foul of this or any other rule, made our order, promptly paying in cash. Strangely this coincided with us receiving our week's wages, which were paid in cash, just in case you didn't finish the next week no doubt.

As we paid for our 'top quality' boots, a nice tidy pile of cash was being built in front of the drill sergeant. At this point one recruit, Neil, couldn't help but eye this large amount, which caught the attention of the instructor who was busy writing against each name the size of boot required. 'What are you looking at lad, my money?'

'No,' came the quick reply.

'Oh yes you were, you were looking at my money, have you got a favourite hospital?'

'No sergeant,' replied Neil.

'Well I suggest you very bloody quickly do, because if you carry on looking at my money like that you'll bloody well need one, because my boot will disappear up your arse to about the fourth lace hole, do I make myself clear?'

Neil very quickly showed that he had a full understanding of what he was being told as he crossed his legs and looked away from the money. All but one of us in the class found this hilarious, in part because it had not been at our expense.

Throughout each of the three stages of training we would all face tests, requiring a sixty per cent pass mark. This led to a final examination at each of the stages and an ultimate exam before being allowed to leave for your Division. You were given another chance if you failed, but it meant that you were put back in the class behind you. After that you would be required to leave and your police career would be brought to an abrupt end. It must be said that the modern recruit, who has far more to learn now, is not treated quite so strictly. Today a young police constable has to learn several databases to be able to cope on the street including, crime reports, intelligence reports and missing people.

Throughout the weeks people would be either pulling out of the training, realising it wasn't the job for them, or in some cases being directed to leave, due to a misdemeanour or failing to reach the required standard.

In our class we only had one casualty throughout the initial three months of training. Her name was Julie, and she didn't seem to get to grips with the studying. To make matters worse she was called out one morning to pretend that she had come across an accident and all she had to do was call up the control room and provide them with the necessary details. She was allowed to make it as gory as she liked, providing she used the phonetic alphabet and the correct radio procedure, which we had recently been shown. The phonetic alphabet is a means to clarify letters over the radio, for example: A = Alpha, B = Bravo, etc.

Julie, with the assistance of her lisp, started. 'Control from PC 123, I have come across a personal injury accident and I am directing traffic in the middle of the A1 . . .'

The conversation at this point was interrupted, loudly of course, as the instructor shouted, 'If you are standing in the middle of the A1 directing traffic my dear you are probably a hundred yard red blotch on the road surface, which some poor soul will have to come and clean up later!'

Apart from the legislation, we were also taken for swimming lessons, which I found a comforting break from the classroom. I have always enjoyed sport, regardless of my ability. Our main instructor for swimming was an ex-RAF fitness instructor.

He quickly explained that whilst the swimming pool was the

property of the Metropolitan Police, he treated it as if it was a member of his own family. He declared: 'I have one particular pet hate and that is dirty bastards who piss in swimming pools. I have approached the senior officers and asked them for a special dye to be added to the water so that when recruits urinate in the pool it will be easier for me to identify the culprit. Unfortunately they declined because some people leak; I'll let you work that one out. That said, I've got eyes like a hawk and if I so much as catch the glint in anyone's eye thinking about peeing I'll have you out of this establishment in ten seconds flat. That will mean you catching your death of cold in Aerodrome Way, waiting in your swimming costume until some miserable wretch takes pity on you.

'Do I make myself clear?' We all acknowledged that he was indeed a most clear communicator.

'Right, who can tell me why your eyes sting when you have been in a swimming pool?' he continued.

'Could it be the chlorine, sergeant?' volunteered one of the girls.

'No it damn well can't be the chlorine, it's dirty bastards pissing in the pool.'

With this we were divided in to two groups, those that could swim and those that couldn't. That is what I liked about the police in those days, everything was kept nice and simple. Of course, those who had failed to learn the art of swimming were told how miserable and useless they were, but they would be swimming before they left training school. Policing may require you to act in many arenas, we were informed. At this point we were told that unless your nearest and dearest fell in the River Thames under no circumstances should we follow anyone into the river because of the dangerous currents.

Over the weeks ahead I continued to enjoy the swimming, nicely falling into the category of not being good enough to start additional training, or sufficiently bad to encourage the attention of our instructor.

One of the girls in our class didn't seem to enjoy swimming that much though, so much so that she managed to avoid a lot of the swimming lessons, which we had about every two weeks. Now I didn't want to know too much detail, but her monthlies had definitely become fortnightlies.

We were shown how to jump into the water from the side of the pool without our heads going beneath the surface and consequently we had to practise this. It would be useful for two reasons, we were told: one, you didn't want to go below the surface of the water; and secondly, you could watch the person you were attempting to rescue. At this point one of the quiet lads was told to jump in, which he flatly refused to do, despite some serious shouting by the instructor; it was nose to nose stuff. With no further ado Rob, a non-swimmer up to several weeks earlier, was called to the deep end.

'Right!' bellowed the instructor as he looked at Rob. 'This moron can barely swim, but he is going to throw himself in to the deep end.' Rob definitely gave a look of 'Am I?' at this stage, but, as the instructor's attention was transferred to him, with no further ado Rob launched himself into the pool with a large splash. Despite this, our quiet colleague still refused to go into the pool, declaring that whilst he could swim he didn't like getting water on his face. I had to take my hat off to him, it appeared to me he had been well and truly covered by the instructor throughout the entire experience. Meanwhile, Rob doggy-paddled back to the side. Eventually the instructor gave up, declaring that the rules did not permit him to drown recruits, much as he would have liked to. It was a rare moment indeed.

Another experience that all the blokes had to encounter was the rigours of boxing. This was to test your 'bottle' for those occasions when you would find yourself dealing with a violent situation. It didn't teach me anything about boxing, other than what side of the ropes to be on. The weekend before the dreaded boxing I went for a lunchtime drink with my dad. One of the regulars at the pub we were visiting had done a bit of boxing and fortunately for me he was there. I very quickly asked what would be the best thing to do if I came across someone who knew a bit about it. I tried not to sound too desperate to know, but nonetheless I was. 'It's quite simple,' I was told. 'You tuck your arms into your sides to protect your ribs, put your gloves up against your forehead and do some bobbing and weaving, no problems.'

We had done some boxing training prior to the big event to prepare us and what I did discover was the fact that the boxing gloves were huge, they were outsize, at least twice the size of the things you see on the telly, and two minutes of hitting a bag left you exhausted, with your arms hanging down by your sides like a couple of clapped out old shoelaces.

Finally we were all paired up and the bouts began. I was paired with Rob, and I could only hope he excelled at boxing the same as he did at swimming, but clearly he was a tryer. That said we both agreed that we would go easy on each other. Of course it came to our turn and we were set off at each other like some illegal dog fight. Rob threw a number of punches, with no success, and I managed to do the same as we bobbed and weaved. I thought I would follow the advice I had been given just days earlier. I couldn't go on much longer before I got a whack, surely, and the instructor seemed extremely keen that at least one out of every bout got a whack.

Without any further delay I followed the advice, but with those ruddy huge gloves I couldn't see a damn thing. I hadn't been given any advice on this at all and like Rob in the swimming pool I was now well out of my depth. Where on earth had Rob got to? I couldn't see him. This was not turning out to be such a good idea after all; in fact, it was beginning to seem foolhardy. Nothing else for it though – I had to move the gloves to see where he was and as I did so I got punched square on the nose. As some of you may know, this immediately causes your eyes to water and I was painfully aware, very painfully, that with the huge gloves and my watery eyes there would be a good chance I would be getting more of the same.

We hadn't agreed on this! Sod all this boxing nonsense. I reverted to simple thuggery and launched myself at Rob. He could have some of his own medicine. Rob backed off and with this the instructor grabbed hold of what hair I had and told us it was the end of the bout. 'It can't be!' I said. I needed revenge, it was only right and proper.

'You can carry on with me if you like,' the boxing instructor offered.

I thought about this very briefly, looking at the instructor. Revenge is a terrible thing, it's rarely thought out properly, so I kindly declined the muscular instructor his kind offer and declared that he clearly knew best in such matters. Rob kindly apologised later, but I had to agree it was my own fault entirely.

Oh dear.

A recruit in another class could always be heard whenever he was about and he was in my opinion too loud all of the time. He was a big lump and declared how he and another other lad would be paired up due to them both being the same height, although 'Mouth' by far and away had the weight advantage. The other lad was a quiet, polite guy and just ignored the comments about his forthcoming destruction.

Sure enough they were paired against each other, but prior to the boxing we had all been asked if we had any boxing experience. Up to the point when the instructor gave the order to start, Mouth was still talking about what and how he was going to do to hurt his fellow classmate. With the whistle to start the bout, the big oaf apparently ran at our quiet chap taking a swing with a large haymaker, which, had it connected, would undoubtedly have caused considerable damage. He wasn't to land his punch though, which was neatly dodged and followed up with a very sharp uppercut that brought a resounding 'Ouch!' from all those that were watching. Before the instructor could bring the bout to an end our quiet man managed to deliver two further blows in very quick succession, leaving windbag well and truly winded and prostrate on the gym mat. By all accounts our quiet man had been a very good amateur boxer before joining the police, which had been missed somewhere along the line.

A couple of days later I was queuing for my lunchtime meal when I noticed, but had definitely not heard, our now not so loud fellow recruit also standing in line, accompanied by a nice black eye.

In addition to boxing, swimming and studying we also had to learn the art of first aid. Our instructor for this soon learned that I would not be his top student. I am not proud to admit that my first aid skills in bandaging techniques fell woefully short of the required standard. After our first test he asked who managed to get ten out of ten. One hand was raised: Chris had until a few weeks earlier been a paramedic with the London Ambulance Service (LAS). The instructor then squeaked if anyone had got nine; no more hands were raised, and neither were there any in the air at eight. 'Right, I've got a right bunch of idiots,' he declared through gritted teeth; nothing to do with any failure on his part of course to teach the subject correctly. Eventually, when he thought everyone had put their hand up, he asked if anyone had been missed out. Up went my hand and I declared that I had only got four answers correct.

'Oh you're one of those clever little buggers that they send to me to get rid of, I shall be watching you very closely indeed.'

Oh dear.

Despite all of this I managed to navigate my way around first aid and achieve the required pass mark. I continued to struggle in future years though, as you will read.

As I managed to get through the first two stages of training school, each being celebrated with one of the few occasions that I would allow myself a drink (and there are a number of stories of disaster at these times), I finally found myself wearing the red and yellow lanyard. My senior instructor at this time always seemed to arrive late for a class but always managed to leave early. I always felt that he didn't want to be there and most of us felt the same – we didn't want him to be there either.

During one lunchtime a few of us strayed over to the gym, when we saw someone clad in full kendo outfit, plus bamboo cane.

As we watched this man go through a number of routines, it was clear to see that he was proficient in his art. He transpired to be our senior instructor, who we also learned was a black belt in karate. At one of his classes shortly after this he called me out in front of the class to carry out a search on him, something that we would regularly be doing for real in the coming weeks.

I knew that I would be unable to find all the articles he had hidden on him and sure enough I wasn't wrong. During this exercise he started to joke at my expense, something that never bothered me and certainly held me in good stead throughout my career. Unfortunately I have always held the opinion that what was good for the goose was good for the gander. This is foolhardy, because others senior to you may think differently, as I was to find out.

At some stage I commented on the nice sergeant's St Michael's tie, to which he commented through gritted teeth, 'Why don't you and I go over the gym?'

At this stage of my life I was reasonably fit. I was about six feet tall, weighing just over thirteen stone. However, there was no doubt that had I gone to the gym I would have needed considerable help to get back, if I could have made it back at all. Again my survival instincts in part deserted me as I looked into the instructor's eyes and said, 'That's very kind sergeant, but I'm not that way inclined.' The class burst out laughing, which only made matters worse. There was another familiar explosion, whereupon I was told I would have to go and see one of the inspectors the next day. It looked like I would be walking out of Hendon before the end of my training.

That night I regularly kicked myself for my stupidity and knew that I was going to get a grilling on all the legislation we had learned up to that stage. Feeling sick I spent a large part of the night revising all that we had learned. I was awake early the next morning and I continued my revision. Fear is a marvellous thing, it can enable you to achieve far more than you would have thought possible.

The next morning as directed I knocked on the relevant inspector's door and he told me that my instructor didn't believe I was going to make the grade. I was then faced with questions on what the various definitions of theft, burglary and 'going equipped' were, as well as what constituted a road traffic accident, to which I provided all the correct answers. Eventually, after more questions, I stumbled on a definition and was told that clearly I had problems and therefore I had a week of lunchtime remedial classes. It was the best thing that could happen, because I did revise and I passed the final exam, much to the consternation of the senior instructor, who I only saw once more some five years later, by which time he was an inspector.

Of course you couldn't leave Hendon without a celebration, it was traditional, and who were we to break with tradition? I had been tricked into looking after the class valuables each time our class went swimming or to do some physical exercise. I was very cleverly caught out by a cunning instructor at our first gym lesson. 'OK,' he shouted, 'who is ex-forces?' Up went several hands, followed by further questions. Who had been cadets? Builders? And then we came to bankers. 'I said, bankers, and I don't want all of the blokes to put their hands up.' Of course I had been lulled in to a false sense of security and found myself responsible for the duration of my time at Hendon looking after the class valuables. This did however assist me on one occasion when I was the last one to join up with my classmates. When we moved around Hendon as a class, we marched, led by our class captain. Mulling around and wandering around in a gaggle was not acceptable and furthermore would not be tolerated.

The same instructor who gave me the job of looking after the valuables asked why we hadn't moved off when I appeared, and of course I was questioned immediately, to which I replied I was always last after I handed the valuables to every team member, ensuring that I completed my duties as he had directed on selecting me for the role. I escaped any punishment and became known as a 'bullshitter'. If you could see my class photograph, emblazoned on the back of it are those immortal words, written by one of my fellow classmates.

That said it was all front on my part. As well as looking after the valuables I had been given the task of collecting funds from all the class in order that we could celebrate our successful passing out. One particular day, we were in the intermediate stage and our instructor came in to find me with only a small pile of cash in front of me, unlike those who sold boots.

He had a good sense of humour and decided to play a little joke on me and I, like a halfwit, fell for it. Having distracted my attention, my cash disappeared off the desk, with the sergeant announcing that I should be more careful with the money. 'It must have blown out of the window,' he said. I, like an idiot, asked if I could go and search for the said money as I didn't fancy paying it all back. How I came to believe this, God only knows, because the wind doesn't suck things out of a window generally and even if our class door had been open the corridor was an internal one and certainly was not a wind tunnel.

Having been given permission, I charged downstairs to look through the bushes for the cash. I was given a few minutes before the instructor told someone to call me back, and I was informed of the above information. I went a deep red and thanked the sergeant for returning the cash, which at least I wouldn't have to replace.

Eventually I booked coaches to take us all to an evening at the Circus Tavern in Essex where we would go and celebrate, and celebrate we did. We all drank a large amount of alcohol, but no one misbehaved in any form. All our instructors were invited, but our senior one couldn't attend, despite my personal invite.

The following morning, much the worse for wear and with my head down I dragged myself out of my block and headed towards the canteen for some much needed protein.

'All right Smithy?' another set of legs asked me, dressed in the familiar blue uniform.

'Yes thanks mate,' I replied.

With that all hell broke lose as my intermediate instructor began to shout at me. I could see he was certainly not under the weather, despite drinking far more than I had managed. His booming Welsh voice I had no doubt could have been heard at the other side of Hendon. 'Just because we spend one night in each other's company Smith, don't think you can get familiar with me!'

In between splutters I managed to tell the sergeant that I wasn't getting familiar, I hadn't recognised him as I was nursing a thick head.

'I'll give you a thick head, get yourself sorted! You have your passing out parade in a few hours.'

Oh dear, he wasn't wrong.

A few hours later, with plenty of water, breakfast and (for me) a rare headache tablet inside of me, I met my family who had come to witness my passing out parade. It was a great day. Despite it being winter the weather was fantastic and I collected my warrant card and even managed to march correctly. I can still remember the moment my photograph was taken as I stood against a particular wall, still standing at Hendon today. My mum kept that photo on a small table at home up to her passing away four years ago.

I had packed my bags ready for a quick getaway, and these were loaded in to my car. Thus I left Hendon and returned home, ready for the next stage.

3

Unleashed on the Public

Having completed the initial training all recruits were bussed to the headquarters of their respective Divisions. At this time each Division consisted of a dozen or more police stations and was run by a commander, a very senior officer and not someone that you would wish to see very often. I still found I had much to learn as our commander sat me and the other new officers down in his office. At this point he informed us all that we would be a burden on him and the rest of his fine officers, because for the next five years he considered we would at best be 'uniform carriers', until we had learned our trade. Despite that, some poor soul had to make a decision at the completion of only two years service whether we were proficient enough to be confirmed in the rank of constable, which he doubted, having read our brief autobiographies, which we had all completed on our first day at Hendon.

It was at this point I realised that the speedy autobiography I had completed fell far short of the grade, a point the senior officer quickly pointed out. 'So I see the highlight of your childhood was visiting the Cubs, whereupon you were asked to walk up and down with a book on your head, which you found boring, so you didn't bother going back. I suppose you are one of those who gives in at the earliest opportunity? Well, you will soon be tested, mark my words.' Further to this he pointed out that Hendon was a stroll in the park and our continuation training comprised fifteen monthly tests.

'What?' screamed a voice in my head. More bloody learning!

How much legislation was there for a beat copper to know, for heaven's sake? The commander must have noticed a far-away look in my eye, because he again concentrated on me, adding, 'This will be followed up by regular meetings with one of my superintendents to discuss your future, if indeed there is to be one.'

Finally we were allowed to leave, where we were taken to our respective stations. My luck here began to change, because I was based at a nice south London station away from the main station and all the senior officers. I found stations like this to be the best places to work over the years, with a far more relaxed atmosphere. Things improved further as the team I was with turned out to be a very nice group of people, headed by a pleasant sergeant. I didn't realise that sergeants could be pleasant. It would be the responsibility of the sergeant to complete regular reports on me, taking into account the marks I got at continuation training to decide if I should be allowed to stay in the job.

Despite having a good sergeant I still managed to upset him on a couple of occasions. Throughout my service I have been late for work a handful of times. My first time was about a year after I joined, when I woke to see that I had twenty minutes to get to work, ten minutes of it being the drive. I knew I was in trouble. Panic ensued, but it never entered my head to phone in sick, you would be letting the team down, so I completed a land-speed teeth-brushing and washing exercise, and I collected a Bic razor from the bathroom on my way out. If I had time I could shave before parade. That was it, I had the answer.

Parade consists of a supervisor who checks who is on duty and posts them to different jobs. In my case, and that of other young constables, this would be walking a beat. If you were fortunate, you would be given a time for refreshments. Additionally you would be given any useful intelligence and times of any other postings for your shift.

Decision time for me: late for parade or forgo the shave. If I was lucky perhaps the sergeant wouldn't notice, I could explain that as it was approaching night duty I intended to grow a beard, I was sure I had read that in our instruction book somewhere. Of course I didn't go unnoticed and my dirty state was quickly noticed.

At the end of parade the nice sergeant (possibly he could have been a training school instructor) began to shout. 'What do you think you're doing turning up like a sack of shit?' At this point, I produced my get-out-of jail Bic razor, discarding the beard-growing explanation. Smiling, I said, 'It's all right sergeant, I have my trusty razor with me,' which I now held up for him to clearly see. Oh dear! I think he may have been overcome at this stage because he just pointed towards the toilets, so I followed the finger.

Now, learning curves sometimes appear to become steeper than you expect, or want them to be. I found this out when I discovered that as we no longer took prisoners at our station the only form of soap was a watery solution, but I had to get on with it. As a young man, with soft skin, I managed to shave easily enough, but this was at the cost of several nasty chunks being taken out of my face. The resulting cuts refused to stop bleeding, and I was eager to get the matter out of the way. I gave in and stuck bits of toilet paper on my face and returned to my sergeant, hoping that I could make fun of myself. I looked a complete and utter mess. That he was not amused would without doubt have been an understatement. No, I wouldn't be having a cup of tea. Yes, I would be walking the furthest beat, and no I could not return to the station at any time that day until the good sergeant had left for the day, because if there was a God he wouldn't see me again that day or indeed any other day. Note to brain: keep thoughts and silly actions to myself. What I didn't tell the sergeant though, was that an aunt and uncle of mine lived on the beat and so I visited them for a bit of respite. You must remain resourceful at all times in the police, oh yes.

Once I was posted to my beat I loved the thrill of taking calls that could result in some excitement. One day a call came out of 'suspects on', followed by an address near to my location. This meant that an address was being broken into. I cut through a small wooded area to get to the address and as I did this I came across half a dozen youths sitting in a huddle who immediately scarpered the minute they saw me. This required little investigation so I called on the radio that I was after the suspects, giving my location and the direction of chase. I wasn't a bad runner in those days and what made it far easier was the fact I didn't have to lug around all the equipment you do today. The modern officer will have a utility belt, with an asp (a type of metal baton that replaced the truncheon after 150 years of good service), CS spray, handcuffs and a torch, plus the very essential stab vest, better known as the 'Met vest'. This is all very cumbersome, despite its necessity.

So I was quickly after the young burglars who had been doing a sort of Fagin before my arrival – namely, sharing out their ill-gotten gains. I was very quickly gaining on them and with the reassurance that my colleagues were on their way I felt confident that we would catch them. My little group jumped over a high fence, so I followed close behind. There was only one problem with this – their local knowledge of this particular area was better than mine. Their drop was the same the other side as where they took off, about six foot. I of course expected the same, but in fact it was nearer nine foot. I landed awkwardly and twisted my ankle, but I knew I hadn't broken anything so I kept after them as best I could. This delay had given them the opportunity to pull ahead again. By this time we now had India 99 above, which also had an operator who worked our ground. If you have seen any of the police programmes with the police helicopter you will know how good they are in these situations.

The youngsters started to make their way through to the main road from the sides of houses. I could see an open back door so called out, 'Police!' as I entered in order to try and cut my suspects off. What instead happened was for me to find a rather angry-looking (not surprisingly) and upset Alsatian. With few options available and one that I immediately dismissed, I dived into the living room and locked the door, looking out of the front window to see if I could spot my thieves. The owner quickly came along and allowed me to exit her home safely as I quickly explained what all the fuss was about. As I got onto the street I found that all of the burglars were being gathered up by various members of the relief who had quickly arrived to make the arrests.

I had twisted my ankle, my arse had nearly been bitten to shreds by a dog and I hadn't even managed to make one arrest myself. Great result, though all the burglars had been arrested and the property was recovered and restored to the owner later. This was why I had joined the job.

4

The Importance of Tea

Now, tea is a very important part of policing. I have been told this on a number of occasions. The first time was day one with my new relief, when our regular station-minder, a PC of considerable years' service, explained that as I was the new boy in the job, I would make all the tea for the rest of the relief. This duty could only be missed if I had an arrest or was dealing with an incident. I was then given the necessary times that I should attend the station to complete this most important duty. My three days with a home beat introduced me to a few of his 'tea spots', which could be useful when I was out on foot patrol. Indeed, I began to gain some confidence and feel as if I would get the hang of this policing lark after all.

When our fatherly station officer went on leave I would find myself sitting in the seat. There was so much to know: how to deal with property found in black cabs; the cost of applying for a firearms or shotgun licence; found dogs; as well as the regular accident reporting and other administrative roles, and of course, good tea-making. It never took that long to make the tea though, as the kettle, which was a huge thing, was constantly on a low gas, ready for the next important brew.

On one particular occasion I found myself in the front office and was feeling rather grumpy about it because policing was about chasing criminals surely, and I was stuck in the damn nick. Having made the relief a cup of tea a call came out on the radio: 'A Dobermann running wild in a back garden, with a young child nearby.'

'You see Sarge, if only I was out on patrol, that would be the kind of job you could send me to, you have to admit, it's ideal for a probationer, but of course I'm stuck in here doing station officer.'

I still hadn't learned from my earlier lessons. The nice sergeant simply said, 'Mick, take the gobby little probationer to the call, where he can act as a bone, and I'll cover the station.'

Oh dear.

One of the few things not to change during my time in the job is the way the Met deals with dogs. We have a dog-catcher, which is a pole about five feet long with a strong piece of plasticised cord threaded through it, which, if managed carefully, will enable you to catch the dog. I have never found this particularly easy. Amazingly, on that day I did manage to catch the dog, only to find I was then placed in the back of the police van, along with the dog. I was beginning to see the error of my ways. Probationers at this time were expendable, there was no health and safety to say otherwise; common sense prevailed, along with a need to get the job done. At best your health was important to somebody else's safety.

During the continuation training days we continued to learn a number of other important things to enable us to be competent in our duty. These included what constitutes a firearm (which is a lethal barrelled weapon of any description, which is capable of discharging ammunition as well as any *noxious liquid or gas*). I had been talking with my sergeant when our station officer, JD, returned having paid a visit to the toilet. Now JD liked his food, and he liked to explain how some of his toilet visits had gone, generally in graphic detail, but I shall spare you that.

On that day, looking at me, he proclaimed, 'Boy, you better give Crossness a ring, they've got a wide loading coming down any minute now.' (Crossness was a sewage farm.) At this stage I pointed out to my sergeant that JD could be considered a firearm and indeed he was committing an offence as he did not have a firearms licence.

'Oh, how is that then?' my skipper asked.

'Well you see Sergeant, JD is regularly discharging noxious substances . . .'

With this the overweight PC grabbed hold of a fire extinguisher while shouting various threats, which involved a number of my body parts and what he was going to do to them. Adrenalin immediately kicked in and I was over the counter, out of the station and onto the high street, laughing. Looking behind me and thinking I had lost my senior colleague I saw in fact that he was not far behind, in fact he was far too close, with a very determined look on his face as he held the extinguisher in his arms ready to deal with me in the appropriate manner. As he ran past the bus stop, the three or four early morning cleaners looked stunned as he bid them a good morning, quickly to continue in pursuit of his prey. Having made good my escape I thought it wise to let JD leave the station before I returned from my beat, quickly grabbing my beat helmet and swiftly making my way back to my regular check of the shops, which I did at the end of most night shifts.

There were two available male toilets at our station, both in the same rest room, although if anyone knew JD was paying a visit he tended to be left in peace and quiet and allowed the entire room to himself. On another of his excursions to the toilets, JD was met with a sign declaring that one of the toilets was out of action. Armed with his daily paper JD settled in. A very short while later he entered the front office, still holding his paper, trousers around his ankles screaming, 'What dirty rotten bastard put cling-film over the toilet, I'll kill whoever is responsible.' Wisely no one came forward. I didn't witness this sight, which was probably just as well – even policing for a few months would not have prepared me for that sight.

Of course, in order to make tea you require a tea club, which in turn requires funds. Ours was run by JD, who made it his duty to collect the weekly fifty pence from each and every member, which he diligently recorded in his book. He would give regular updates on the progress of the club, but the club we were informed had entered dark times. His report in the station book read, 'It is with great sadness fellow members that I have to report we have a thief amongst us. I have tried to shield you all from this, but for some weeks now several pints of milk have been opened at the same time, with the culprit taking the cream off the top of each and every pint.' The message further stated that if anyone knew the name of the culprit they could leave it in JD's tray in order to protect the identity of the informant, whereupon JD would deal with the matter in his own formidable way.

Despite this warning that he was on the case, the offences continued to take place, until some weeks later we all received an update titled: 'JD solves the riddle of the old cream nicker'. Now JD could best be described as rotund. His report read:

> Fearing for the future of the tea club and with members becoming disgruntled at the theft of the cream off the top of the milk, the ever-diligent JD, having tried numerous methods to halt the crimes, decided to take action. Early one morning the *sylph*-like JD entered the canteen, turned off the lights and secreted himself behind the kitchen door. It only remained for him to be patient before the culprit would show himself. Time went by, but he would not be deterred from his duty and remained at his post, just like the diligent officer that he was. Eventually, footsteps approached, yes they were coming closer. Breathing in slightly I steadied myself as the kitchen light went on and the fridge door opened, whereupon not two but three pints of milk were opened, with the valuable cream being skimmed from the top of each into a bowl of porridge and bananas. At this point, with sufficient evidence, the swift of foot JD apprehended the culprit in a vice-like grip; yes I can reveal that the thief is none other than that thieving bastard Fruit [another long-serving officer]. Sentence has been passed and his last four weeks' tea money

has been doubled, with no time being allowed to make payment. I have shown mercy however on this miserable wretch and allowed him to remain a member of our prestigious club. PS: There are a number of other defaulters who are overdue this week, who will also be receiving some special JD attention.

We had one WPC on our team. The modern Police Service no longer uses the 'W' to indicate a women officer. Prior to Carol arriving at the station there had been few female officers at the station and it had only been in recent years that they had been allowed to do night duty (though long before I joined I have to say). Now Carol, it was assumed, could cook, why, she was a female, isn't that what all women did? Now, the modern politically-correct world would have something to say about this, but nonetheless, it is fair to say that Carol indeed was a fine cook. The old copper would generally make the best of any situation. In this case it was traditional to have a relief meal on night duty. Why, they now had a cook, so it could be an even better event than ever before.

On her maiden meal, Fruit (forgiven for his earlier cream theft), at the end of the meal made his excuses to leave the table in order to retrieve his pipe, which seemed odd because he was rarely seen without it. All became very clear when he left the canteen, closing the door behind him. Shortly after this there was what can best be described as a very loud fart, or 'botty burp' as JD would call it. Shortly after this, Fruit innocently returned to the canteen, clutching his trusty pipe for all to see, unaware that his attempt at gentlemanly conduct had not gone unnoticed. With this JD shouted, 'I don't know why you left the canteen to fart Fruit, that could be heard at the other end of the high street.' It was at least a start to the introduction of gentlemanly conduct inside the nick as the station began to crawl forward slowly in order to join the modern world.

I always enjoyed night duty. These would be the times you

would chase a stolen car, or wrestle a violent husband away from the family home. Despite this, tea duty still called. One evening I returned to the station at the allotted hour, as I had been directed. I was also required by my sergeant to have another good reason to be in the station in case I should need to provide an explanation for my attendance. As I entered the front office our superintendent was seated next to JD. I now knew what the sergeant meant.

'All correct sir,' I said quickly. This was a familiar way to address any senior officer at that time and for years before and since.

'Is it? I'll be the judge of that,' he challenged.

Now, there were not many reasons a senior officer would be up late unless there was trouble and I wasn't aware of any, unless, as on this occasion, he was the 'late senior'. This meant he would be visiting all the stations and checking the books to ensure they were correct.

'What are you doing in the station anyway?' I was asked. He was clearly aware of my true reason, but I explained that I had a number of stops, which included one young lad who I wanted to investigate a bit further with the intention of conducting further enquiries immediately I left the station. 'Forgive my manners sir, but can I make you a cup of tea, while I am here?'

Of course even his years of service would not result in the decline of a cuppa. Off I ran to make the tea and a little while later I presented him with his tea, white no sugar, as directed. With this he looked at me and said, 'Don't give me my tea first lad, no you should look after the station officer first.'

'Oh he likes his tea to brew a bit longer sir,' I replied.

With this the superintendent looked at JD and said, 'I can see this one has been under your wing. Now you can get back on your beat.' Which I did, happily, minus my own cuppa.

Later that shift I returned for my mealbreak but before I did that I checked on JD to make sure all was well. He congratulated me on having a suitable answer for the boss as all well equipped officers should. As most of the relief were back at base and having missed our earlier tea, JD announced that he would make the drinks and to celebrate we would be having a milky coffee – pure luxury, could life get any better than this? I was given some rare respite from my tea-making duties and kept my sandwiches back to enjoy with our treat.

JD loved his grub, no not just loved it, adored it, couldn't wait for his next meal, it was like watching someone eager to see their sweetheart again, too much time away was too painful to bear. My first introduction to JD and his love of food also came in one of my early night duties when I popped in to make tea (again) and was asked to cover the front office just for a moment while JD retrieved his 'cow pie' that had been put in the oven some time earlier. He quickly returned with what can best be described as a family-sized casserole dish, a completely full casserole dish, with something resembling a shepherd's pie in it. 'Well go on then boy, make the tea. I'll need something to wash this little snack down with.' Off I toddled and a little while later I returned and the rest of the team had settled into the chairs scattered around the front office, waiting for their drink. With this JD let out a burp, and put the lid on the remaining uneaten half of his 'cow pie', with the promise that he should save himself now otherwise he would be hungry later in the night. This probably wouldn't have been the case if we'd had the 'twenty-four seven' eating establishments that are now available. Boy could JD eat.

5

A Day in the Life of a Probationer

The first time I visited the superintendent I went to his office, and again a regular went with me – better known as fear – and that well known feeling again of the familiar clench deep in the tummy. I was directed to a seat at the far end of the office, where the boss could have a good look at me. My experience has shown me that when a senior officer asks a question, a large percentage of the time they already know the answer. On this visit he discussed my first three continuation training visits. Each of the visits had seen me just about attain the necessary sixty per cent. 'You know what this tells me? he asked. I didn't need to reply. 'You are a slacker, you are doing the minimum to get through. If you didn't have ability you would have failed. In three months you will be sitting in front of me and we shall discuss how you have fared in those visits. I don't want to see any marks in the sixties young man, off you go.' I didn't need to be asked twice to leave as I left with sweat covering my brow.

The warning helped me though, for on my first visit back to continuation training I managed to get in the high seventies, followed by a slightly lower mark at the next visit. I clearly had this licked and so I rested on my laurels for the third visit, when I got sixty-nine per cent.

Oh dear.

The superintendent probably had several set speeches that he would have used for probationers, but he certainly recalled our previous meeting, congratulating me on taking heed of his words

31

and picking myself up, but clearly I had not followed the same rule for the last visit. He told me that he expected after the first two visits I would rest on my laurels. Bloody hell, he must be a ruddy mind reader. A very clear warning was given that this would not be tolerated at our next meeting, or else. I didn't want to ask what the 'or else' was – I knew it wouldn't be good. Sure enough the next three visits, accompanied with my now familiar friend, fear, I managed to keep out of the sixty per cent marks. Thank you dear God.

The early days of being sent out onto the streets as a young in-service constable was certainly a daunting experience for me. Nothing but questions would go around in my head. What would I do if . . . and what if this happens? The thrill of the job though was going to work and never knowing what you would have to deal with, and while the exciting parts were what you yearned for there was also a fair amount of boring duties.

One particular shift I was working with another team, when a call came out on the radio: 'Urgent assistance required.' This meant that a police officer was being threatened or assaulted and needed help immediately. Such a call would see canteens empty, differences between officers being shelved as everyone made their way to the location as quickly as possible. On this particular day as the police car had barely come to a stop I jumped out of the panda to see another probationer I knew, Darrell, who was being chased by a fat drunk, who had managed to take Darrell's truncheon off him. Darrell, in fear of his safety, did what Forrest Gump was to do years later and kept on running, until the violent drunk was tackled to the floor by a couple of old sweats, before taking him to the station. You would be regularly reminded of these types of incident and have to sit there as the event was replayed, with each telling becoming more exaggerated. It was a great way to divert your attention away from some of the less pleasant incidents.

During those early years you certainly learned who to seek advice from and who not to. One Christmas I was posted on a panda, with Phil, a recently Hendon-trained police driver. Keen to show his prowess at the wheel we took off at speed to the call of a disturbance. Upon our arrival there was a lot of shouting at a flat, between a brother and sister, both in their thirties and old enough to know better. I asked them both to calm down, which they did and I asked what the problem was.

Of course the arguing began again and eventually I explained that if they could not agree to calm down completely I would be forced to make an arrest to prevent a breach of the peace. With this the man, who was wearing a large coat and thick glasses, explained that we would get another call back. I explained that I didn't want to ruin their Christmas, but if I had to I would be forced into making an arrest, which is exactly what I had to do. Throughout this Phil kept giving me the evil eye, clearly unimpressed with my softly-softly approach. Now, at this time police officers did not carry handcuffs, although a pair was kept on the van and area car if there really was a need.

As we got to the street the man asked if he could get some money off his wife, who had been quiet throughout the incident, as he would need to get back home in the morning. I had no problems with this as the man had been fine with us throughout. Phil on the other hand told me to grab hold of the bloke and just put him in the car. Despite still being a probationer, I told him the guy wasn't causing us any problems, why should we be any different?

A little while later we arrived at the charge room and after booking him in I took the man to the cell to obtain details that the court would require the next day. With this my friendly prisoner removed his large coat to reveal a huge set of biceps and even bigger shoulders. He then explained how his thick glasses had got him bullied as a young child and his dad had told him to toughen himself up or put up with it. Several years of judo and karate had seen him get black belts in both, nicely followed up with some weight training in between times.

This led to him doing some door work at nightclubs. One unfortunate night a gang of five started on him, resulting in all five requiring various forms of hospital treatment and he got a charge sheet with five offences of grievous bodily harm (GBH). At this point Phil had secreted himself by the cell door trying to mouth to me that the Police National Computer (PNC) had flashed that our prisoner was violent. Oh really. After bidding the prisoner a goodnight, I chatted with Phil and pointed out that had I tried to manhandle the prisoner into our car, both of us would be eating hospital food through a straw.

Reporting crimes clearly took up a lot of your time, particularly for a probationer who would learn their trade reporting the more mundane offences. We used to carry the crime sheets with us, which only required some topping and tailing upon your return to the station, getting a crime number and letting the control room know the result – job done. The modern officer has to return to the station and complete a detailed report on a computer. These machines are like feeding infants and they always have a hunger for more information, which is fine, but this is the case for very minor offences as well as the more serious offences. They are however fantastic when you are researching criminal activity on your ground.

The rules for completing these reports were quite simple. Fill in all the necessary blank boxes neatly, including the informant and victim's details, address and what property had been taken or damaged. Additionally you had a small box to explain how the offence had occurred. In the case of a burglary this would usually go something like, 'Victim one left their first-floor flat locked and secured. Upon their return they found the front door had been forced with a blunt instrument and the property listed removed unlawfully, with no witnesses.'

As I walked to the crime desk one morning the two old sweats who managed all the minor crimes called me over. I was ordered to read a crime sheet and as a probationer was asked if I could understand the example, which had been photocopied and placed on the wall beneath a sign which read: 'How not to do it'. The example I was directed to had been completed by Dermot, another probationer on my relief at an adjoining station. The old sweats wondered if I, as a probationer, could understand the mind of a likewise young in-service colleague; clearly we were all like-minded dimwits that Hendon were knocking out.

Dermot's crime sheet went something like this:

Victim one owns a first-floor flat, which he shares with a friend on occasions, who is the informant. Victim one went on holiday (see the dates above) and left the keys with the informant who used the flat at some point but cannot remember exactly when. He subsequently decided to go on holiday himself, which victim one had been unaware of prior to his departure. Not knowing what to do with the keys the informant passed them on to a joint friend who gave them back to the informant upon his return, but prior to the return of victim one. When victim one returned he found out about the burglary and decided to report that his property had been taken, but is unsure if it was taken at the time of him originally leaving the flat or after the informant left the flat, which he will confirm later in case the joint friends can confirm if they had stayed at the flat, which occasionally they do. He can confirm that the property listed was definitely taken, although there is now a dispute between the victim and informant over who owns what. [Answers on a postcard please.]

Dermot also had a very unique way of making tea, at least as far as I was aware it was unique anyway. I witnessed this early one morning when he kindly asked if I would like a brew, which I quickly accepted. The next thing he filled up the large metal teapot with cold water, threw in a handful of tea bags and dumped it on the gas stove. On production of some steam he declared the brew ready and rather reluctantly now I accepted my cuppa. My sense of foreboding was not amiss, it was bloody awful. How on earth had he been allowed to get away with this for all these months? JD would have personally killed me if I had made so much as one like that. It certainly does take all sorts.

The early-turn shifts certainly took some getting used to. A 6 a.m. start never held a great appeal to me, particularly if I had been out the night before with some of my mates, which would invariably result in only a few hours sleep. I just assumed that as I got more service I would adjust. One morning I was to go out with a recently transferred officer whom I met in the canteen. Tony had twenty-six years' service at the time and he often drove the area car (these are the fast response cars you see flying around with lights and sirens blaring). Tony sat at the table with his head resting on his arms. I enquired if he was all right, which he confirmed, saying he was just grabbing some shut-eye while he could. With this I said, 'I suppose with your length of service you get used to these early morning starts?'

In a typical old sweat style he raised his head off his arms, looked at me and replied, 'Are you some sort of c**t?' Over the years this incident came back to me on numerous occasions, even more so as I approached my own twenty-six years of service. Tony wasn't wrong!

The canteen was always a good place to go; although at my station you couldn't buy a meal, it was a case of a home-made sandwich, a bag of chips or else resorting to reheating the night before's leftovers and not in a microwave either – they hadn't arrived on the scene at this stage! This particular late turn I arrived at the head station for our area, where the canteen could supply you with hot food from early morning through to seven in the evening. I joined the queue, which was rather large, as the canteen staff efficiently took our orders and swiftly produced our meals.

As a probationer you would stand quietly waiting your turn. That evening, all of a sudden, Geoff, an old sweat area car driver pushed his way to the front of the queue, shouting that probationers should know their place, needed to show some respect and make way for those with service. As he began to write out his meal ticket the canteen hatch was lifted and out came Elsie, all four-foot ten of her, armed with her mop. 'You cheeky bleeder, get to the back of the queue!' And with this, in a typical *Dad's Army* style, she began to go through some bayonet routine (Corporal Jones would have been proud), with Geoff backing off to the end of the queue as directed, proving Corporal Jones's point: 'they do not like it up 'em'. Mission completed, Elsie returned behind the counter, exclaiming, 'That's exactly what the bloody Jerries would have got as well if they'd bleedin' landed I can tell yer.' She must have been well in to her sixties at this time and was loved by all the station. Despite this, Geoff seemed to get his dinner ahead of the rest of us and was later seen driving Elsie home, which was a regular duty, whenever policing duty permitted.

You quickly learned about the regular villains and other characters that would be attracted to the station by the ever-present blue light outside. This would include those suffering from harmless delusions, busybodies and well-meaning members of the public. We had one regular who was well intentioned, but was like a dog with a bone. I believe at some point she had suffered a breakdown, but she was a fit old bird and well capable of looking after herself.

Whilst I patrolled the high street I found myself engaged in conversation with her, which included the various misdemeanours of the local neighbourhood, when she directed the conversation towards those who failed to pay their road tax and the burden this placed on the state. Strangely enough she thought their cars should be taken away and crushed. Not that daft was she? Anyway, with this she spied a car with no tax displayed, whereupon she threw herself into the road in an effort to stop the vehicle. I immediately grabbed her and pulled her from the road, with her telling me off for not doing my duty. I managed to calm her down when I explained that I had got the number and would visit the driver at a later time.

Upon my return I explained the incident to JD, who was always keen to guide me in the right direction and provide invaluable input in order that I could improve in the future. On this occasion a scream came out of his mouth. '*What?* You had the opportunity to deal with a simple accident that would see the scourge of this station not to darken these doors for months and yet you saved her?' He was flabbergasted briefly before following this up with some explanation about me pleasuring myself in a sexual way. You can't please them all.

Oh dear.

JD was certainly very professional when he dealt with people, but his patience could be pushed. Another regular was an elderly lady who paid him a visit one particular morning and explained that she was outraged because all of the locals thought she was a prostitute.

'Well if you are a prostitute, my dear, then all I can say is you should go down to the Social, because you must be living on the bread line.'

As a young copper I always seemed to find myself chasing people. I had a good record of catching them, it was great fun, and even better when you made a good arrest. Of course there had to come a time when I wouldn't make the catch. It happened in the middle of a night duty. Nick and I were dealing with a regular who was about to get himself arrested when another car pulled into the garage area where we were. There was a very quick squeal of brakes as the car was put into reverse in order to make a quick exit. In his panic the driver stalled the car so I immediately began to run after it. There was another quick attempt to start the stolen car but it wouldn't budge, so the driver's door flew open and we were off.

I quickly began to gain ground on my new-found friend. Nick put the call up on the radio and it was game on as we ran along the back of the estate. At this stage I was only five or six yards behind him. After a few hundred yards he turned a corner and ran up an incline, but he had begun pulling away from me at this point. As he went round another corner there must have been about twenty yards between us and as I followed him around the corner the area car screeched to a halt.

My suspect had disappeared and the only place he could have gone was a nearby block of flats. Oh I searched and I searched but

I didn't find him. I had seen his face and I would remember it, but I never did see him again. I was furious. I had been so close. Yes, we had recovered the stolen car, but he had got away. Probably my pride was dented, but it wasn't right, this shouldn't happen.

When I got home three or four hours later I still hadn't come to terms with the loss of my suspect. My dad was already up having a cup of tea and asked me how my night had gone. 'Bloody awful.' I told him the whole sad story. With that I changed into my training kit and despite my dad telling me I was nuts I went for my regular five-mile run. When I had finished I still wasn't tired, I had to get it out of my system. When I got back indoors my dad asked me if I felt any better, which I didn't.

Still not happy with myself I got my swimming trunks and thought I would go and tire myself out in the local pool. I wasn't thinking straight at all at this point and found that the baths didn't open for another thirty minutes or so when I got there. I was too restless to wait so I went back home.

'Happy now?' my dad asked.

'No, the bloody pool wasn't open.'

'You know you won't catch them all over the next twenty or thirty years, there will be others that get away, you'd better get used to it.'

I knew he was right, but I didn't like it.

After a cup of tea and a bath I went to bed, doing a rather good impression of Grumpy out of *Snow White*.

In my last couple of weeks of probation I was posted, as all probationers are, to a CID attachment. During this posting our detective chief inspector had received news that a local Co-op was going to be held up at gunpoint. Today there are risk assessments done for just about everything. In the days of *Life on Mars*, as you will know if you have seen the programme, it was done differently.

With no training I was armed with a white overall, clipboard and pen. I now only had to look as if I knew what I was doing. Some years earlier I had been a Saturday boy for Tesco, so I was made for the job. I didn't give any thought to the fact that I might be shot. Further armed with all this naivety I wandered around until finally it was called off; probably just as well.

Today you would have had the specialist firearms unit discussing with the local superintendent and the robbery squad all manner of things before a large document would have been completed before they got anywhere near the street. I am not knocking this at all, far from it. It just shows how the world has changed since I started.

There have been a number of incidents over the years where the Met have been criticised following firearms incidents. The Met alone deal with thousands of incidents each year. The officers undergo a lot of training and the senior officers are trained to manage such incidents. I don't care what anyone else says: the Met are excellent at this sort of thing and they take it very seriously indeed.

At the end of my probation, the new commander decided that all probationers should transfer elsewhere on his area and experience another station, so we would have to up sticks and move. I really hated this idea; you were settled with your team, they could trust you to do your job and you were beginning to know your ground. Despite this I would have to move.

Oh dear and oh bugger.

6

Mental Health Issues

I honestly believe that the police deal with those suffering from mental health and harmless delusions in the best possible way, mindful of the fact they have loved ones. I have already mentioned a couple of incidents relating to this subject earlier.

A few years out of my probation at another station an elderly lady visited in the early hours of the morning, complaining that she could hear voices coming through the walls and they wouldn't leave her alone. Another old station officer called her into the front office and told her that he had a cure, but she had to promise that she wouldn't tell anyone, as it could reduce the effect. With this the old PC put together a number of paper clips to form a necklace and whispered that if she kept it somewhere safe and if she ever needed to block out the voices, she only had to put it round her neck; to his knowledge it had never failed. With this the lady took her new necklace and happily left the station.

A few years later the daughter of the lady visited the station, explaining that her mother had recently passed away. For a few years she and her family had been woken in the early hours as her mother complained of the voices, when the calls suddenly stopped for no apparent reason. One day, rather reluctantly, her mother explained why she no longer needed to phone in the middle of the night. She explained what the necklace was for and how she came to get it, but under no circumstances could she tell anyone else. From that day on her elderly mum had slept in peace, along with the rest of the family, and the daughter wished to leave a note to thank the officer, who she didn't know. His kindness had resulted in her mother's final years being so much more pleasant and comfortable.

I was sent to an address early one morning as the section sergeant, where a psychiatric team had a warrant to take a lady into care under the Mental Health Act. When I got there I was given the update by the attending psychiatrist and he was adamant that we had to get her out. If necessary he wanted us to carry the woman out of her flat. With this the PC who attended the call in the first place, Christine, raised her eyebrows at me to get my attention. I explained to the psychiatrist that I would do my best and would investigate the matter. I immediately spoke with Christine who told me that we wouldn't be carrying her anywhere. This was quickly confirmed when I went into the living room to find a very large lady of some girth, only about five-foot three tall, but of considerable weight. If we had to carry her the officers plus the lady would not have fitted through the door.

'Hello,' I said. 'Now can you tell me why you won't come to the hospital for a short while so that we can get you checked over?'

'I'm not going anywhere with him,' she replied, pointing at the doctor who had now joined us in the living room. I have found this on a few occasions: despite the fact they are suffering from mental health issues people quite often know who the doctor is, either from a previous meeting, or from instinct.

After a short conversation she began to thaw and told me her name and where she had lived. I then brought the conversation around to food (clearly and correctly I thought this might be a passion of hers). 'What are your favourite foods?' I asked. With this she began to go through some of her favourites. I asked her to wait a while as I had a quick discussion with the doctor and then returned to our lady. 'I have just confirmed they have one of your favourite meals tonight. If I promise you that, will you come with me?' With the doctor out of sight she took hold of my hand and like a child walked to the waiting ambulance, checking that I would keep my promise.

On another occasion as a sergeant at another station we were called to another female who again had to be taken under the Mental Health Act to a nearby hospital. The LAS were already on scene but the lady was refusing to leave her home. I was with my duty officer that night and the lady was very pleasant all the time the LAS or we spoke with her. We had to wait for the psychiatrist to arrive who apparently had the necessary paperwork.

When he got to us I began to speak to him, but he just waved his hand at us stating he knew all about the case and didn't need any help from us unless he asked. With this he went straight into the address and began to speak to the lady. As soon as she recognised him she slapped him across the face, knocking his glasses off his head. My duty officer went to assist but I held him back explaining in the hearing of the psychiatrist that the gentle-man had a clear understanding of the case, far greater than ours and he would ask for our assistance only when he needed it, which he quickly did. A short while later we accompanied the lady with the LAS to the nearby hospital.

Those suffering from mental health issues are often a danger to themselves as they feel they have run out of options. I have been to a number of calls where such people have threatened to jump into the River Thames because they have had enough. Quite often this results in their bodies being recovered by the Marine Police Unit (MPU) days or weeks later. One such call that I attended was at the top of a building with the man standing on a small ledge, the wrong side of the balcony rail, with officers attempting to talk him down. He would not have made a pretty sight had he jumped.

The London Fire Brigade (LFB) attended and began to rig roping up on the floor below to take the man off the ledge if necessary, but they were obviously careful to ensure that if they took action none of their officers would be falling with him, if all else failed. When I got to the officers they had done a sterling job keeping the man from throwing himself off. At one point though he decided to attempt the jump and three of us managed to get a hold of anything we could as we struggled to hold his weight, about fourteen stone of it. As I held one arm I thought, 'You bastard, you have now transferred this responsibility onto us,' as I looked down twelve floors below where he would soon be heading. Fortunately the LFB were able to drag him to safety from the floor below.

On another occasion on an early shift I was in custody and a young man had been arrested the night before for doing slam dunks with his body on the roofs of cars. This had resulted in several cars being badly damaged before the police arrived to take him to the station after a violent struggle. What concerned me was the fact that the officers who told me he was immensely powerful were not weaklings themselves.

Our forensic medical examiner (FME) attended and stated that we needed to get a medical assessment of the man and he would return once a psychiatrist was there, which took place some time later. The psychiatrist demanded to go into the cell to do a proper assessment of him. I asked if he could at least try first through the opening of the cell (the 'wicket'), or with the door open slightly, but he wasn't having any of it. I got a few officers into the charge room as I opened the cell door.

Our man was now sitting cross-legged in the corner of the cell grunting like an animal. He was now dressed in just shorts and T-shirt, with his huge arms on display. We slowly entered and the prisoner walked forward on his arms, grunting all the time. As he got near us he grabbed hold of the ankle of one of the officers and began to pull him back into the cell, grunting like a wild animal with his prey.

Despite the officer trying his best he couldn't break the hold and had to allow himself to be dragged into the corner of the cell, just managing to stop himself from falling over. The psychiatrist very quickly got out of the cell, which allowed us some more room as I told the man if he didn't let go of my officer I would be forced to hurt him before he could get off the floor. I wasn't kidding, this guy was clearly very ill, very powerful and very dangerous. I did a bit of weight training at this time, but I had no doubt that I would make a very poor second if he got off that floor.

Whether he thought I was kidding or not I don't know, but he released the officer and we quickly got out of the cell. He would stay there until the Territorial Support Group (TSG) arrived some hours later after we charged him and sent him to court. The court could decide if they wished to make an order for him to be placed in a hospital for a mental health assessment or not; I'd had enough of this.

In the meantime the psychiatrist and I had a little chat.

These calls do not always end badly as I witnessed one early shift. I was directed to deal with a call of an elderly lady found wandering at a local shop. Oh blimey, it would take ages to find out where she was missing from, I thought.

I quickly arrived to meet the shop assistant who had called us and she explained the lady was in her nineties and was a bit muddled. I went over to the lady who was well dressed and appeared at first glance to be fit and well.

'Hello,' I said. I introduced myself and explained that I was there to act as her taxi for the afternoon and enquired if she fancied coming out with me in my police car.

'You're a cheeky sod, I'm not that bleeding daft yet. I came out of my house this morning and thought I would go for a couple of gin and tonics. When I came out of the pub I had intended to take a few things back home with me. I got side-tracked and then I took a wrong turn, so instead of making things any worse I came in here and this nice lady sat me down and gave me a cup of tea. Once I get my bearings I shall be fine.'

With this she expressed her thanks to the shop assistant and off we went in the panda. Very quickly she identified a local shop and knew exactly where she was. During our little chat it was clear that apart from becoming a little bit disorientated she was in fact pretty sharp. I followed her directions and within a few minutes we arrived at the bottom of her road, which was a short hill. I began to turn into her road so that I could drop her off at her door.

'Stop, stop here. For Gawd's sake don't pull up outside my front door, I have a daughter who is in her seventies now and she's too old to deal with police cars pulling up outside the front of the house. Thank you very much dear for helping me.'

With this she was out of the car and making speedy work up the hill to her front door before the neighbours could make anything of it.

7

You Can't Please all the People all the Time: Complaints

Having mentioned Tony the area car driver earlier, it's probably sensible to explain how he got to our station in the first place. It was certainly unusual for someone with twenty-six years of service to be transferred. Apparently it had been for his own protection, following a disagreement with a local villain on one too many occasions at his previous nick. His management decided it would be in his best interests if he was moved. Tony loved driving the area car and was a proactive copper, who could best be described as a 'thief-taker' by his fellow officers.

Day one at our station he very wisely parked his car outside the front of the station, complete with all his uniform in the back. As the road was marked with a yellow line he obtained permission from the station sergeant to park there, whilst he began to make several trips back and forth to carry his uniform into the station. The nearest car park was well known to the local thieves and sensibly Tony didn't want his car being damaged and a report being completed on the theft of his police uniform.

In between trips a call came out for a van urgently to assist with a violent prisoner. The station sergeant swore as most of the team were giving evidence at court, including the van drivers. Tony, still keen despite his unwanted transfer, offered to assist, with no financial recompense, just to be booked on at that time, which would at least allow him an earlier finish to his day. Quickly someone was found to direct him to the call as he grabbed the van keys and a personal radio.

Approximately thirty minutes later Tony returned with the prisoner in tow and returned the van keys and radio, before going back to the task of completing the transfer of his uniform into his new locker. As he got to his car he found that a parking ticket had been neatly placed on his windscreen.

Oh dear.

A few enquiries traced the traffic warden who was very apologetic, but explained that the chief inspector had directed her to do it, despite the fact she had pointed out the car was clearly owned by a police officer. The chief was having none of it and the ticket was completed correctly and placed on the offending windscreen.

Tony went berserk. Tracing the chief inspector's office he barged straight in, ticket clenched in his fist. With no introductions Tony enquired if he had been responsible for the ticket, which was confirmed with a nod. With no further ado Tony went into overdrive, bringing the rest of the station to a halt with heads appearing from doors all along the corridor.

'You f***ing, useless wanker. If you had half a copper's brain you would have enquired with the station officer, whose permission I had got in the first place. Secondly, you would have discovered that I volunteered to collect a violent prisoner, something you no doubt know little of. Thirdly, if you had any balls, a pen and half a brain you could have written the ticket out yourself.' The chief inspector (wisely) sat in his chair as Tony produced his warrant card and threw it onto the table. 'Furthermore, you know what you can do with that, ask one of your coppers for directions if you don't, you tosser.'

With that Tony stormed out of the office, slamming the door hard behind him, leaving the chief inspector pale and clammy. First-aid instructors would no doubt signal this as possible signs of shock.

A few weeks later Tony showed me his 163, which related to the incident. A 163 is a form that every officer is served with whenever a complaint is made against them. It was certainly very detailed, all two and a half pages of it (most don't even make a second page). In addition to his lack of professionalism, he was further accused of failing to book out the van and the personal radio.

A little later Tony was called before a discipline board. A discipline board comprises of three senior officers who act similarly to a court. Tony saved them the bother of a hearing though and pleaded guilty to all the offences as charged. The full facts were delivered speedily along with details of his previous service history, including receiving a medal for bravery, and various commendations. The board took a short break before deciding that he should be fined one day's pay, for failing to book out the van and personal radio, which were valuable Metropolitan Police equipment.

'Do you have anything to say officer?'

Of course he did.

'Thank you sirs, it's the best day's pay I have ever earned.' He was quickly led away before further action could be taken.

Tony was familiar with complaints. As a busy policeman he managed to collect a few. One that he was particularly fond of related to a rather loud, obnoxious gentleman he had stopped for a driving offence. Tony attended the senior officer's office, where he was formally informed of the allegation that was read out to him. This particular complaint read that the officer had looked at the complainant in a 'menacing and threatening' manner. As with all complaints, after reading out the charge the senior officer would then caution you, similar to that procedure observed in the charge room or custody suite after a person is charged with a criminal offence. On this occasion Tony replied, 'Guilty as charged.'

The senior officer said, 'But you can't do that to members of the public.'

'Oh I think you'll find that there is nothing to say I can't and I am also guilty of such behaviour regularly with all other arseholes, and there is nothing in any of the books that says I can't, unless it's just been changed. Good day sir.'

When I joined, an uncle of mine asked me not to pick on the

poor motorist. I like to think that I kept that promise, although that didn't stop me from being sensible in my approach without neglecting my duty. I don't know the figures but I should imagine before the advent of speed cameras and local authority parking wardens, police officers probably upset the public more by reporting them for a traffic offence than anything else.

An officer I knew called Len spent several years in the Traffic Division and probably would have stayed there longer, but for a meeting with a central London mayor one day, who would not accept that he was in the wrong. The mayor apparently made threats of reports to senior officers and later complained that the officer had told him to 'f**k off'. As a result of this Len was returned to his old stomping ground.

When Len tells this story he informs you that he was found guilty of the wrong offence: it wasn't 'f**k off', but 'bo**ocks'. When he got to thirty years' service we celebrated after a late shift with a couple of beers. We had a small presentation which I made. In the short presentation I informed him that there was someone who wished to send his congratulations but unfortunately the mayor couldn't make it that evening. His reply was indeed 'bo**ocks' and not as charged. You can't win them all.

I heard one interesting story which began in a custody suite one late shift. A prisoner had been brought out of his cell to speak with his solicitor. When the young gaoler began to escort the prisoner back to his cell a violent struggle began, with the custody sergeant the only other officer present running to assist. During the struggle one of the officers managed to hit the alarm, knowing that this should bring some assistance pretty quickly, but it didn't come. The struggle continued for a couple of minutes until an officer returned with his notes from an earlier arrest. With the prisoner tiring and with the help of the other officer they managed to overpower the man and lock him back in his cell.

Immediately the sergeant made enquiries to find out why there had been no assistance and confirmed with a test of the alarm system that it was not working. The fault was quickly reported and a radio quickly obtained should something similar happen later. The police doctor was called and the officers, plus prisoner, were all examined. After each examination the doctor made the relevant entry in the official book.

Police doctors are paid by the police when they carry out any work, and they remain true to their oath. They do not side with the police, merely record what they see and do. They also make a decision whether the prisoner is fit to remain in custody, or needs hospital treatment. When I first joined the 'docs' were known as 'divisional surgeons'. This of course changed, but nothing is ever shortened in my experience so they became known as forensic medical examiners. Such a title deserved an acronym, so they became known as FMEs.

A few weeks later the custody sergeant was called to see the chief inspector to collect his 163. As usual the complaint was read out, which simply stated that the sergeant had used unnecessary force. After the caution the sergeant replied, 'I have a reply, it is quite lengthy, so when you are ready sir?

'I agree with the allegation, as charged. I think it only fair that I inform you that I hold the senior management of this station entirely responsible for failing in their duty to ensure that the alarm strip in the custody suite was not working correctly and I have confirmed that this had not been done for some time. If the system had worked correctly assistance would have attended the custody suite far quicker, enabling us to overpower the prisoner quicker and saved him from the amount of injuries he did incur. I must further state that if the MPS are taken to court on this matter I would consider myself a prosecution witness as I believe the prisoner has a case.'

The chief inspector was lost for words, so the sergeant signed for his copy of the 163 and left, stating that he could not talk any further on the matter and advised the chief inspector to obtain advice from the Police Federation as he believed he would benefit from some good advice.

Oh dear, that didn't go to plan.

Whilst I was a sergeant one of the regular jobs would be to relieve the posted custody officer for a mealbreak. On one particular morning I visited the custody suite and so I asked my colleague, Alan, what would be the preferred time, duty permitting. As we were discussing this matter Alan handed me the 163 that had been served on him the day before. The allegations against him were of kidnapping and unlawful imprisonment, although Alan didn't look too bothered.

He informed me, 'I got a bollocking when I collected that. After the guv'nor read out the allegation I told him that these were very serious allegations and I should be sent home immediately on gardening leave, just like senior officers are, when they are in trouble. He threw me out when I told him my garden needed doing and this was a good time of the year to get on with all manner of things. I was just trying to think out of the box. Anyway, what about relieving me at about nine o'clock for grub, that'll be smashing, it might take my mind off of this.' As I left him to his own devices he seemed to be concentrating more on whether to go for the bacon or the bangers.

Years later, when I was an inspector, I found myself in a custody suite about to do some reviews of prisoners one early shift. The duty inspector has to ensure that each prisoner is being dealt with as speedily as possible, taking in to account all the other rules and regulations. As I prepared to do this a young lad of about 19 had been charged and the sergeant was restoring his property before bailing him. As the lad took his property back he threw his property bag across the room and was then escorted out of the station.

Minutes after he was released I was informed that someone wanted to make a complaint against the police of the theft of a fifty-pence piece. Now this is a silly amount of money but the allegation is serious. Usually I would make a complainant wait at least for a short period in order that they can calm down. Most of the time you are in the middle of something and they have to wait anyway. On this occasion I had a good idea what had happened, so I immediately went to the front office where I confirmed that it was the young lad who had just been released and asked him what he wanted. He was still angry about being arrested and explained that he wished to make a complaint of theft. I didn't say anything about what I had witnessed, but clarified it was a fifty-pence piece that was missing. I asked the young man to follow me back to the charge room where the property bag was still lying in the corner of a room. At this time all charge rooms had been fitted with CCTV, which was also accompanied with a large poster informing everyone of this fact when they entered the room. I picked the young man's property bag up, opened it up and saw a fifty-pence piece at the bottom. I asked the young man if he could confirm the coin was in the bag and restored it to him.

I then pointed to the large CCTV poster on the wall and clarified that he could read without any difficulty, which he could. We then went to my office where I explained that all his actions had been captured on the CCTV system and if there had been any wrongdoing it would have been recorded. In fact he was lucky I didn't give him a fine for wasting police time to add to his troubles.

Fortunately on this occasion, because I had witnessed the events, I was able to save a lot of hassle as there would have been a need for officers to have been interviewed, which would also mean them being away from patrolling the streets. The CCTV would have to be reviewed anyway, all because of something very silly. I pointed this out to the young lad, informing him that he had already signed as accepting his property back and just because he was angry making a silly complaint wouldn't help his cause. Of course police officers are not always in the right, but what other profession has as robust a complaints procedure? Certainly not solicitors and lawyers or MPs, yet they are, at the end of the day, just a reflection, like police officers, on the make up of the society of the day.

8

Wind-ups and Bored Policemen

At about the same time I was completing my probation, JD had decided to retire, having completed twenty-five years' service. At this time officers could get a half pension if they left at this point, but this was stopped a few years later. In fact anyone who joins the police service today has to serve thirty-five years before being eligible for their pension. JD was a larger than life character, so one of the other characters (there was never a shortage) devised a cunning plan to see him off in a suitably fitting way. At this time, JD, who was always thorough in his duties would check every MOT presented at the station against a list of stolen certificates, which was kept near to the station office desk.

On his final day a nun entered the station with a HORT/1 (this is a form a police officer issues to get drivers to produce their driving documents). A lot of people know it simply as a 'producer'. Upon production of her MOT following her accident and according to the form, JD, still being diligent as everyone knew he would be, checked the MOT against the list, to find that it was indeed a stolen MOT. He couldn't believe it – on his last day he was faced with having to arrest a nun, and there was no one else around to get to deal with this extremely delicate matter.

In his best voice he pointed out to the nun that the document had been stolen and it would require him to investigate the matter further, which could only be done at the charging station. As he began to cite the caution, the nun asked if there was any way she could avoid such an embarrassing situation, to which she was informed that would be totally improper. There was only one thing left for the nun to do, and she began to strip off and show her well-formed body to a once-and-only totally gobsmacked JD. He later explained that this couldn't possibly be happening to him, but all became clear when he was quickly joined by the rest of his mates. JD quickly recovered though, and asked the strip o' gram if she wanted to finish the job as she was only half way through. The stolen MOT was returned to the property store where it had been borrowed from an old case.

In the early days of my service, my fellow probationer Dermot was the victim of a wind-up by one of the sergeants. He informed Dermot that there had been a dangerous spillage of chemicals in the Thames and every station where the river ran through their ground had to get a sample. Dermot was reasonably quick to ask to see the message, which was produced by the control room staff, who had completed the message an hour earlier. Today everything is computerised so this would not be so easy to do.

Dermot had to book out a huge set of waders and gloves as well as a specimen bottle normally used for the drink driving procedure, with specific instructions what to do. He was further informed that as there were dangers of there being a toxic incident he had to be left on his own, so that this would reduce the number of casualties! Dermot didn't seem to mind that it was toxic and the fact he had to go on his own. Once he collected the sample he called to say that the mission had been accomplished, to then be told that there had been an update and he had to go back and do it all again, but to collect the water sample from at least six feet from the shore. All the relief watched as he did this and congratulated him on the safe collection. In truth I think the sergeant believed he was going to fall in.

Years later at another station a similar ruse was used again involving the great river. On parade on the eve of the night in question I read out to the relief that there was to be an experimental security operation the following night involving the police helicopter, India 99. The helicopter had to fly along the river and at certain stations carry out a number of tests, which could not be divulged at this time. It would assist the operation if the officer chosen had previous knowledge of helicopters, but not essential in case any jargon was used. With this, Nick put his hand up, explaining what we already knew, that he had been in the forces in New Zealand, from where he originated. He arrived at our station when the *Crocodile Dundee* films came out.

'Why should I choose you then Nick, what skills do you possess, I don't want to let the operation down, I won't even be here tomorrow, I'm in custody, so I need to be reassured.'

In his familiar New Zealand twang he gave a brief résumé of his understanding of how a helicopter operated and his previous involvement whilst in the forces. I established that the rest of the relief were not more experienced before I gave Nick the job. Everyone else was already aware of what was being prepared.

The following evening at the appropriate hour I was informed that Nick had been taken to his rendezvous point (RVP) and I was able to listen to the proceedings on the radio. Our duty officer had also sanctioned this, so we had the green light. What I was even more amazed at though was the fact that the Information Room (IR) had also agreed to assist.

IR called up the station and asked for permission to have talk through with the officer who had been deputed to assist with the operation. Before our station had time to acknowledge IR, Nick eagerly came on to the radio. 'Yeah MP, that'll be me, I can confirm that I am at the RVP and awaiting further instructions.'

Nick was told to stand by as IR had to use a secure radio link to talk to India 99, before coming back to announce that India 99 was only two minutes from the destination. At the prescribed time someone purporting to be the India 99 operator informed IR and our station that they were now above the RVP and asked for a direct link to Nick.

'Go ahead,' beamed Nick. He certainly did seem ready for any challenge.

'Nick, we are hovering a considerable distance above your

current location, can you confirm that our engines cannot be heard from your location?'

'India 99 from Nick. I can confirm that I cannot hear your engines, as per the operation you would appear to be in stealth mode.'

'Thank you for your assistance Nick, we also need to check some other equipment that we have had installed for this operation, we are now going to use our new thermal imaging cameras from our current height to confirm if they are working correctly, can you confirm that there are no obvious signs of other people, particularly large groups, in your immediate vicinity?'

'I can confirm that there are no obvious signs of anyone else around at this time.' This was good as it confirmed that the rest of the team were well hidden.

'Nick, our machine may be malfunctioning, are you able to do some star jumps to increase your body temperature in order that we can confirm your location, we are not picking anything up at all at the moment.'

With this Nick began rigorously jumping up and down, throwing his arms in to the air, to raise his body temperature. As something of a keep-fit fanatic this could have gone on for some time before he was interrupted and asked to stand still. Another twenty or thirty seconds went by before he was informed that there did indeed appear to be a fault with the machinery.

'Nick, clearly at our current height we shall have to report back that the machine is not sensitive enough. Are you able to remove any of your uniform so that we can see if that has any effect?'

Sure enough, despite it being cold, Nick took his uniform off to reveal a bare torso, which he confirmed to India 99. With this they confirmed that the machine was still not working and thanked everyone involved as this allowed the engineers some time to rectify the problem before a secret operation took place in the very near future. With this IR and India 99 thanked Nick and the station and declared the operation complete.

The reality of the ruse was quickly brought home to Nick when the relief began to appear from a variety of nooks and crannies. He later turned up at the custody suite where he told me he thought better of me and of course he had indeed thought it was a wind up all along until IR called up, quickly followed by India 99.

A few years later, Nick became a home beat on a busy run-down housing estate. Not long after he arrived there the local kids found out his nickname and asked him how he came to get it. Nick, without a second thought, said in an emphasised Australian (no doubt recently adopted) accent, 'You seen those films called *Crocodile Dundee*?' To which all the kids shouted, 'YES!' 'Well I don't like to brag too much but much of that shall we say relates to some of my previous work before I emigrated over to here, but don't tell anyone.' 'WOW!' they all shouted, and suddenly feeling in awe of a now local hero they all immediately ran off to their respective homes to update their parents.

Just before Nick left the team we dealt with an arrest and were about to make our way back to our own station. As we got to the yard I suddenly remembered something so I began to run back to the nick. As I got there I shouted, 'Give me two minutes Crock!'

With this my superintendent, 'Boycie', appeared and said, 'You know that nicknames are a forming of bullying don't you?'

'No sir, I don't.'

'Yes it is. I was on a course recently and they informed me that whilst we all think nicknames are humorous, you don't know the effect they have on the person themselves. Often they won't say anything because they feel intimidated, or feel the need to put up with it in order to feel part of the team.'

Well I could understand this in a primary school, but we were in our thirties. It certainly wasn't meant as bullying.

'Well, think on what I have said.' And with that Boycie noticed one of the other members of the team and hollered, 'Badger! I need to see you in my office, two minutes, OK?' ('Badger' got his nickname because of a birthmark on his head, which was a different colour to the rest of his hair.) The superintendent looked at me, oblivious to what he had just done and said. 'Well, remember what I've said and ensure the rest of your team are aware also.'

'Yes sir,' I said in a daze, almost lost for words as he walked back to his office to speak with Badger.

Wind-ups can also backfire. The home beat who took me out for a few days before I was allowed out on my own recounted a story when he had still been on team a few years before I joined the job. The plan was simple: one half of his relief were going to water-bomb their colleagues once they had finished their mealbreak in the early hours of the morning. They waited patiently as their colleagues came into the station for their break. Ray could see a shadow coming towards the back of the nick where he had carefully positioned himself and quickly launched his water bomb with great accuracy. Unfortunately he had done this without realising who his target was, which transpired to be 'Big Karl'.

Karl was about six-foot two tall and weighed about twenty stone at this stage of his life. He had been the MPS undefeated wrestling champion for years and was also very good at martial arts. He once told me that he had never done any weight training in his life, apart from every morning when he lifted his duvet off to get out of bed. He didn't need to do any weight training though; he was naturally very fast, despite his size, and very strong

Ray, realising the mistake he had made, ran as quickly as he could and jumped in to his panda, making sure that he locked himself in it. Karl gave chase but was too late to get Ray before he took shelter in the Austin Allegro. Before Ray could start the engine to make good his escape, Karl lifted the front of the car up and informed Ray that it would be best if he got out of the car unassisted, in order that there was not a lot of writing to do to explain any damage to the patrol car.

Ray dropped the keys out of the window as directed and handed himself in to the custody of Karl, who lifted all fifteen stone of Ray up off the floor, held him against a wall and told him that he should be more careful in future as bad things could happen to bad boys. Towards the end of the warning and to emphasise the warning even further, Karl began tapping Ray gently in his chest with his index finger with the arm that wasn't now holding Ray off the floor. Apparently it was one of Karl's' party tricks. Fortunately for all us coppers, Karl was a gentle giant and a true gentleman, unless you wished to play rough games. Karl could be very good at rough games.

After I had taken parade early one morning Ray informed us all how some half-wit had managed to drive into him on the way home after early turn the day before, leaving a nice dent in his car. Ray explained that it was that bad he had called the police, such was the nature of the driving by the other driver. Moaning about his poor fortune he finished with a comment along the lines of, 'I shouldn't be surprised if I don't get prosecuted, instead of silly bo**ocks.' During the course of the day he sought advice from our team inspector, who reassured him that he had taken the correct course of action.

A couple of weeks later a letter arrived via our despatch system addressed to Ray. He was on holiday at this time so the envelope was opened as per instructions and inside was a letter informing Ray that his accident had been fully investigated and it had been decided not to take any further action against the other party.

Len decided to make a photocopy of the letter and change some of the wording, which he managed to do quite skilfully. Remember, this was the pre-computer age and the work was done on a typewriter and photocopied again. The letter was then delivered to Ray with a new date once he returned from holiday. He hit the roof. The expletives would take a page to get close to covering what he said. His blood pressure must have been close to a dangerous level and the air was most definitely a bright shade of blue.

Eventually, when he was calm enough to talk, he updated the team with the news that he was to be prosecuted for failing to supply details of his insurance when requested to do so by the other party at the time of the accident. 'Didn't I say something like this would happen? I was the one who called the police, they're not doing anything about matey boy yet they're saying *I* may be prosecuted and they want *me* to contact their unit to make an appointment to discuss it all!'

As it was 6 a.m. in the morning we still had a few hours to let this run before the relevant department opened with Ray looking for blood. Ray announced that he was going to see the duty officer – he had after all discussed it with him on the day, and he would back up his story. As Ray drove over to meet the duty officer I was informed of the update as I was covering the custody suite that day. I informed the duty officer who was in his office just around the corner from the custody suite. If the letter had been correct there would have been serious discipline issues facing an officer in such circumstances.

Very quickly Ray arrived and discussed the matter with the duty officer, who called me into his office to act as a witness. Ray was asked to go through the story again and the duty officer denied ever saying that Ray had taken the correct course of action after the initial accident. Ray was looking completely deflated and lost. To make matters worse, the inspector added, 'If this went to court Ray, I couldn't say that I recall the conversation you just mentioned. What do you think sergeant?'

'Well sir, clearly this is a serious allegation. I would suggest, Ray, that you contact your Federation representative and arrange for them to accompany you to the interview. Of course you will have to complete a full written report on the circumstances for the chief superintendent.' I have never been very good at this sort of thing, I usually get the need to break out in a fit of giggles, but I managed to control myself.

Ray looked at the inspector again, and then the inspector said, looking at me, 'Do you think we should tell him all of the facts?'

'Yes sir, I suppose that we should really.'

Ray looked at the inspector with a puzzled expression. The

inspector then told him that it had all been a wind-up. Ray exploded again, saying it was only because the inspector was a senior officer that he didn't call him 'a no good fu**ing bastard' and stormed out of the office. You could say he was relieved that he wasn't being prosecuted but he was a little more than upset with his colleagues, who were told so when he caught up with them.

One wind-up that I particularly enjoyed occurred one day when Darrell (still with his truncheon) and I were both posted to a small police office. We had just started our early shift and as we were patrolling, Darrell began to tell me about his latest conquest. Darrell could be quite graphic about these events and God above knows what the public thought with some of his replays involving him thrusting his hips out like a pneumatic drill and replays of his arms rolling all over his tunic in some pornographic mime act.

Anyway, as we were walking on our beat he began to tell me he had met a young lady who had recently split with her long-term partner. 'She was obviously in need of a shoulder, so what could I do?' Darrell asked. 'She needed comforting, at least while she was on the rebound.' Apparently the young lady had been living with her partner for a few years in her apartment, her partner being a six-foot four builder, and built like the proverbial outhouse.

The events of the previous evening went something like this. Darrell was in the bedroom with the young lady, giving her a shoulder to cry on (I shall spare you the details that I was given). What a gentleman, who said chivalry was dead? All of a sudden a key was heard in the front door. Darrell now began to show me his scared face – it looked impressive. He then explained how he quickly jumped out of the bed threw open a bedroom window and managed to shin down a drainpipe, hurdle a wall to the safety of his car and drive away . . . quickly.

'You were bloody lucky Darrell, by the sounds of things he would have killed you.'

'Killed me? Killed me? This bloke is bloody enormous by all accounts and the reason they split up was partly because of his jealousy. Killed me? That would have been the best I could have hoped for.'

A couple of hours later we had returned to the police office for a cup of tea. Whilst Darrell was making some room for his tea I told Taff, our station-minder, very quickly about Darrell's little incident and asked if he could think of a suitable wind-up, and left it at that.

A short while later Darrell and I were back on our beat when he received a call on his personal radio from Taff.

'Darrell receiving. Go ahead Taff.'

'I've just had someone on the phone trying to get hold of you. It was a poor line and I couldn't make out all that he was saying, something about building work, you're having some building work done?'

Blood was draining out of Darrell's' face very rapidly. I knew enough about first aid to know, not for the first time, that my colleague was displaying signs of shock. I was beginning to get better at this first aid after all.

'Sorry Taff, what do you mean "building work"?'

'I couldn't hear all that he was saying Darrell, it sounded like he was at the bottom of a barrel of beer or something, anyway I told him you finished here at four o'clock and I did hear him say he would see you then.'

Darrell didn't collapse, but it wouldn't have taken much to have pushed him over at this stage. He looked at me and in a panic-strewn voice said, 'You've got to help me. It's him, it's him, he must have found out after I ran off, oh f**k what am I going to do? What am I going to do?' He was grabbing my arms at this stage. 'You *must* help me, you're bigger than me, please, you've got to protect me.'

I really wanted to break out in to fits of laughter at this stage, but I couldn't, I mustn't, I was beginning to enjoy this too much.

'Steady on Darrell, why should I get all the pain, when you've had all the pleasure? Besides, you heard Taff, the line was bad, don't worry about it, we'll sort it all out when we go back to the station for grub.'

By the time we returned for grub the rest of the team were fully aware of what was going on, including our sergeant. Darrell didn't want anything to eat, he was feeling unwell. I do know this: it wasn't love sickness. I had been catching up on my first aid again.

Darrell questioned Taff further about the conversation but was still very unsettled about the situation and told Taff that he wasn't having any building work done to his flat, and oh dear this looked serious. Immediately our sergeant appeared Darrell requested the last hour as time off.

'Hang on a minute Darrell. Right, the rest of you, we all need to re-parade here at two o'clock this afternoon, I have just seen the superintendent and he wants us to carry out a roadblock and check on the drivers' documents. Apparently all the stations have got to do this and send a return of the results for the next few weeks. Back to you Darrell: you can't have your time off mate, we need everyone to get out there and make a good impression. I don't want to upset the boss.'

'But you don't understand Sarge! I need that time off, it's urgent.'

'Darrell, none of your close family members have died, or if they have you have kept it a closely guarded secret, so for this once you will have to get on with it, whoever she is she can wait for an hour. I shall see you all back here at two.'

Darrell did look ill. He managed to stay with me throughout the rest of the shift until we returned to the office as directed. As the sergeant began to explain where we were going and what we would be doing he looked at Darrell and asked if he felt all right because he was looking very pale.

'I wouldn't mind an hour off as I said earlier Sarge, but you've already refused that.'

'So I did Darrell, would that have anything to do with your builder friend who is coming to see you at four, whose bird you've been shagging?'

As the penny dropped Darrell's face showed a number of expressions in quick succession, resulting in him calling me a person with dubious parentage. He looked a very relieved lad though and back on our beat, having forgiven me, he started to discuss what he was going to be doing and who he was going to be doing it with that night.

Some people just never learn.

There is no doubt that if there was a chemical formula for policeman and boredom, the two added together would need to carry some very severe warning. In my experience I have found that it can only lead to one thing: mischief. I think the mathematical formula would look something like, boredom + policeman = mischief.

When I began in the job the Information Room (IR) was based at New Scotland Yard, and dealt with all the emergency calls; every single 999 call requesting police was answered by them. With the advent of the mobile phone and the police being required for far more things, this has changed and there are now three call centres for the Met.

When IR received an emergency call they would transmit this across the R/T set, a radio that was fitted to only a few cars at each station, including the area car and the van. Today only a few cars do not have this facility, as well as mobile data terminals (MDTs) to receive calls. As an operator, when you accepted a call you would inform your colleagues on the personal radio of a violent disturbance in order that they could also attend the call, which they might not be aware of for a few minutes until the message was sent through to your control room.

If your station was quiet you would listen to others taking calls that sounded exciting and you hoped that you would be able to respond to a call soon, even if it was off your ground. On rare occasions in the early hours of the morning the entire Metropolitan Police District would fall in to a period of quiet calm, with no need of its police officers to respond to calls. When this happened IR would be required to announce on the radio using their call sign of 'MP' to all units that the system was working correctly. I can't even remember where I heard this next story, but I would have enjoyed listening to it. It was of course one of those less busy nights when a quiet voice was heard on the radio: 'I'm a happy little bunny.' Operators at IR failed to take the bait and seconds ticked by with no rebuke, when another operator informed the rest of his Met colleagues that 'I'm a happy little bunny too.' Seconds ticked by and still no response, then another voice confirmed that he was also a very happy bunny, immediately followed by another.

With this the airwaves were broken by IR. 'This is the chief inspector at IR, all units will follow correct R/T procedure at all times. IR out.' Several seconds went by, when across the R/T set came a little voice: 'Oh dear . . . he's not a very happy bunny at all is he?'

Around this time officers had personal radios, which were far less reliable than their modern counterparts. On those occasions when a station went quiet, you would hear the metal clip at the back of the radio being twanged as the transmit button was depressed. This would infuriate the control room staff and supervisors alike. On occasions the control room would inform all units that they had taken matters in to their own hands and turned the transmit button off. This meant that the control room would be the only people who could hear any transmissions that were made. Generally this would resolve the problem.

Many years later I was a duty officer at a station, when the team were not sufficiently occupied and a similar game took place. For a while I ignored this, until I got bored, so I walked into the control room and asked the controller to let me know the next time it happened and to identify the culprit. This was now very easy to do as the radio number would be displayed on a screen as a transmission was made and could be very useful if an officer required assistance.

I hadn't got out of the control room when there was a repeat performance and Steve, the controller, informed me of the young PC at fault. I immediately called him up and asked him to come and see me in my office.

'Certainly,' he replied, 'anything in particular sir?' To which I answered: 'Now, I have confirmed it was your radio number for the previous transmission. I shall leave you to work that out and we can discuss it upon your arrival.' I always repeat to youngsters what I was told: knowledge is power. There is very little chance that an old sweat would have been caught out so easily.

A shy young female officer who was a probationer at the same time as me was sent on an urgent call one night. She must have been about 19 and six stone; dripping wet. It is important to remember that when we began with the job you patrolled on your own and you didn't have any protective equipment. The male officers had a pretty useless truncheon, the girls had an even smaller one so that it fitted in to their handbag, and the radios were not as good as their modern equivalent.

Her task on that night duty was to patrol the back of all the shops which ran parallel with a railway line. This particular area was extremely dark and the noise carried. Anyone of a sensitive disposition would not feel comfortable at all in that environment. It was not all bad though; the Met at this time issued all new officers with a two-cell torch, which I would estimate at its maximum ability was equal to two-candle power, if it was working correctly. Mine lasted a couple of weeks and I quickly found that it was as useful as a chocolate teapot. The demise of my torch came when I rested it on a table while I went to make the tea (how unusual) and it rolled off with a dull thud as it hit the concrete floor. I've never seen anything like it. From just a few feet the bulb, glass and holder had all cracked. It appeared as if it had been dropped from a great height. It was good I suppose because I had to get something that worked like a proper torch.

Back to our young lady though. She had been patrolling for a little while when she made her way up a wrought-iron fire escape to check the back of the doors to the shops as directed. As she did this a tailor's dummy fell off the roof of one of the shops as she approached. It was neatly dressed but also had a rope attached to its neck. The shout could be heard for miles, and was quickly followed by her footsteps meeting the wrought-iron steps as she ran for her life. There was no reply to the calls on her radio from the sergeant who had engineered the whole thing. As usual there were a number of witnesses to the incident who found the incident extremely funny.

It was probably the same dummy that was used one early morning in the old charge room. One of the duties of the sergeant taking over in the charge room is to check that all the prisoners are accounted for and, most importantly, still alive. This particular morning, 'Dumper', a sergeant on my team, had used his tailor's dummy again, only this time it was dressed like a vagrant and hanging in the cell. As his relief came on duty he quickly ran over what prisoners were in and then stated he had to get a quick getaway. Of course this was no problem to the early-turn sergeant who then began to check on her prisoners. She got to the relevant cell and there was an almighty scream and an even larger yell, when she discovered the wind-up. She was seen very quickly running out of the station at a very fast rate to catch up with Dumper, who had last been seen laughing loudly to himself before getting in his car and making a speedy exit.

9

Court, but not Only When You've Been Caught

Well, if I thought I knew what fear was as a young probationer, I still had plenty to learn, as I found out on my first appearance at the local Magistrates' Court. I was accompanied by an experienced officer who gave me good, sound advice. 'Follow your notes, address the magistrate as "Your Worship", answer truthfully and if you don't know the answer, say so.' Fortunately, the defendant pleaded guilty to the few minor traffic charges and I was guided through by a lovely magistrate, who was clearly aware that I was new to her court.

Many of the following tales I learned from canteen talk and no doubt their telling has been exaggerated by the number of times they have been told, but I make no apology as I think some of them are a fantastic insight to the game of chess between the defence and the prosecution that regularly takes place.

The defence have a simple job to do: you shouldn't take it personally. They pick holes in the prosecution to show a court that their client could not possibly be guilty as charged and this often requires an officer being discredited in some form or other, or possibly the officer has misconstrued the view of the incident from the angle they had been standing.

The old-style copper would attend court in their best tunic, in many cases with a number of ribbons on their left breast, depicting medals earned in the forces, along with a police Long Service Medal, which is earned after twenty-two years' service. Many of these old cops would stand confidently in the box, making eye contact with the jury, judge or magistrate.

One particular old traffic officer explained how he had witnessed the defendant driving in a fast and furious manner and estimated in his many years of experience that the driver must have been doing in excess of 40 mph in a 30 mph zone. He corroborated this later by taking the police car around the same journey to confirm the approximation of the speed.

As expected the defence solicitor (or 'brief' as they are often known), clarified the officer's expertise and years of experience once again. This was going well for the officer – all the questions had been clearly answered – when all of a sudden the defence solicitor threw a pencil across the court. Addressing the officer, he said, 'And in your experience officer, how fast was that pencil going?'

The officer looked towards the magistrate, tucked both thumbs into the top of his tunic, puffed out his considerable chest, and replied, 'I am afraid to say Your Worship that I have not been trained in and have no experience in chasing pencils and cannot provide an answer to the gentleman's question.'

A similar occasion related to an officer identifying the suspect from the registration number of his car. In an effort to dispute this, the defence brief questioned the officer on the lighting at the location, the weather conditions at the time and the distance between the officer and the vehicle. Still unable to throw doubt on the prosecution, the defence asked if the officer required spectacles for any reason, receiving a negative reply, when the officer met the final question. 'Just how far can you see officer?'

In a dream-like voice and gazing to the ceiling of the court the officer replied, 'Oh Your Worship, on a clear night I can see the stars.'

A lot of police time is taken up dealing with shoplifters, and there are an abundance of them. One of my earlier visits to the local court brought me to the lovely magistrate mentioned above, who was extremely thorough, Ma'am Long. This day the defendant was an Italian man who stood in the dock with his right arm in a sling. The charge of shoplifting was read out, to which the defendant, replying through an interpreter, pleaded guilty. He looked very depressed. At this stage the defence solicitor took to the court and explained that it had been a moment of madness and with little English his client took flight upon being challenged. In his haste to get away he dropped the items and quickly looked left as he got to the generally busy main road. Unfortunately he wasn't home in Italy and the car travelling from his right knocked him over, resulting in his capture. 'All he now wants to do Your Worship is return to his beloved family and put this all behind him.' As this was being said the Italian male shrugged his shoulders, shed a few tears and looked thoroughly disappointed with the whole incident. The magistrate kindly thanked the solicitor for assisting the court and agreed that indeed he should be returned to the bosom of his family. A small smile appeared on the solicitor's face, before the magistrate finished with, 'But we should send him back in the condition he left them. I should think three months should see his arm fully mended don't you? Thank you.'

Ma'am Long by all accounts was an animal lover and whilst I was waiting for one of my cases to be called I caught the end of a hearing with a prosecution by the Royal Society for the Protection of Cruelty to Animals (RSPCA). The defendant had been charged with mistreating his dog. After considering the case the defendant was found guilty and the magistrate was informed that he was of previously good character. She pointed out to the defendant that she disliked those who mistreated animals, particularly as it was a choice whether to have them in the first place. The defendant interrupted and told the magistrate to 'just get on with it', and no doubt being informed of the relatively small powers available to her in such circumstances and his previous good character, for her to do her worst if necessary. 'Oh I shall,' came the reply. 'Unfortunately it's only three months, take him away.' At this point his legs buckled as he lost his balance and bravado and he was led away muttering in disbelief. You should be careful what you wish for.

Of course things do not always go the way the police officer would like them too. One traffic officer had dealt with a violent situation, which resulted in the arrest of a male for threatening and abusive behaviour. At this time the offence was contrary to the 1839 Metropolitan Police Act. As well as describing the man's violent behaviour, the officer added that the male had told people to 'f**k off'. On this day the court was being presided over by three Justices of the Peace (JPs). On these occasions you invariably experience a number of breaks as they would take advice from the clerk of the court, who would be a qualified solicitor.

After this deliberation the JPs returned and declared that they had come to a verdict. The chair explained that in this day and age the word 'f**k' was an everyday expression and the officer should have taken it as such. Consequently, for that reason, the gentleman was found not guilty and allowed to leave a free man. The officer, none to impressed with this, returned to the station to get some lunch.

That afternoon the traffic officer was back in the same court on more comfortable ground. This time he had reported a motorist for failing to maintain his exhaust system. During his evidence the officer explained how an exhaust system worked and that the gases had to travel through the exhaust, but due to a large hole just before the silencer the gases were escaping and causing a large amount of noise, which was the reason the officer's attention had been drawn to the car in the first place, so he stopped the motorist as permitted by Section 163 Road Traffic Act 1972. The officer was clearly not going to be undone by any silly oversight on this occasion, because it was the same bench who had heard him earlier that morning. Despite this, he hadn't managed to completely get the morning fixture out of his thoughts. At about this point one of the JPs asked how large the hole was in the exhaust, to which the officer replied, 'Oh fu**ing big Your Worships, must have been at least an inch square.' At this point another adjournment was taken as the court inspector was called and the officer was disciplined, resulting some months later in the loss of one day's pay.

Oh dear, oh dear.

One of my first days at Crown Court was as a result of arresting a local villain for driving whilst disqualified. The rules on this have changed since this episode, but Michael and I were always bumping into each other. Unfortunately for him, that had been about two previous occasions for similar offences and two visits to the local police station. He was a likeable rogue, but would go on to bigger things in later years.

That particular night I had been posted to the area car. As mentioned before, the area cars are the fast cars that you see responding to incidents and it was certainly fair to say that the area car drivers were held in some esteem by young officers such as me, and it was with great enthusiasm on the rare occasion that you got to be the operator.

As we drew up at a set of crossroads late one evening I noticed Michael, who ducked down behind the steering wheel of a friend's car and made off. I jumped out of the car, presumably to stop half a ton of car, as he sped away. At this time, because I had not arrested him immediately, I had to apply for a warrant and I arrested him later, which resulted in him being charged and bailed to court. He elected to take the trial to Crown Court, which was his choice at that time.

Along with my now familiar friend fear, we both waited outside the court as the driver of the police car gave his evidence, until I was eventually called. As instructed I addressed the judge, who always appeared imposing until you had been to court several times, as well as looking to the jury, to show them that I was being honest and sincere. Of course, after the easy bit was over the defence brief took to her feet and asked me the usual questions about the area, how could I be sure it was her client, etc. At this stage I had to be mindful that I did not mention I had arrested Michael before as this would have been prejudicial to her client and could have resulted in her asking for a mistrial. Eventually she got me to describe the location, which I explained was well lit with shops on each corner as well as street lighting, with a hill running between the roads the police car had been in, and another hill, facing the road opposite, which was the direction that Michael had been coming from.

At this stage she asked me if I could recall if the front of the police car had the word 'police' written on it. At the time of the incident, the commissioner of the day had decided that we had to change the colour of police cars from blue to white, with a nice jam-sandwich stripe along the side. Certainly the old-style cars did have 'police' on the front, but the new ones didn't. For the life of me I couldn't remember. I certainly didn't want to guess, particularly as the police driver had already given his evidence, so I explained this.

'So, officer, looking directly at your vehicle, which you say you can't remember the colour of, anyone facing your car would have little or no idea that it was a police car, is that not right?'

Oh bugger, she was right, I was going to have to admit this, which could weaken the case, despite the fact I was adamant who was driving. At this point I answered, 'Yes, Your Honour, that is correct,' accompanied by a smiling defence barrister. 'But,' I continued, 'it definitely did have a big blue light on the top of the car though.' With this the barrister offered no further questions and returned to her seat, giving me a glare as the old sweat R/T driver sat smiling at me.

At another magistrate's court I waited whilst the end of another case was being dealt with, again being deliberated over by three JPs who resembled an elderly afternoon coffee group and began to show that was probably the best place for them. This was a simple case of a man who had obtained four brand-new tyres from a garage and made off, without making any attempt to pay. The young defendant pleaded guilty, and representing himself, told the court, 'What do you expect, me girl who I've got a baby with don't give me no money, so there was nothing else for it, but to scarper.'

Clearly showing no remorse my colleagues and I expected some suitable consequences for the defendant. After another break the JPs returned and the elderly chair of the panel told him that he really shouldn't do such a thing and the court had no option but to fine him and this would be in the sum of . . . £10. Len, who was sitting next to me, said far too loudly 'Ten quid? Ten quid? I wouldn't mind a set of four brand-new tyres for ten quid.' As I ushered Len away he further pointed out that the owner had not even been given compensation for his loss, as the defendant asked for time to pay. No one ever said it was a fair world.

At the same court on another occasion Len accompanied a member of his team who was of mixed heritage. Pat spoke with an oriental accent, which was not surprising as English was his second language, but it was easy to understand him when you worked with him every day. After he had given his evidence and been allowed to leave the court, Len took the stand, eager to take the oath and get on his way home. Before this could happen however the court interrupted him and said, 'Officer, before you take the oath, can you just confirm the name of the previous officer please.' Clearly they had not been able to follow a great deal of the evidence and would rely heavily on the evidence Len was about to provide.

When Pat made one of his first appearances at court, no doubt with my friend fear in tow, he was asked by the usher if he wished to take the oath, or 'affirm'. Obviously the court usher was unaware of his faith, possibly due to his Asian appearance.

Pat, always willing to be helpful replied, 'I don't mind, whatever you want, whatever you want.'

'No, I mean are you C of E, or do you wish to affirm?'

'I don't mind,' repeated Pat, now becoming frustrated, despite his offers of help.

After the magistrate managed to calm himself, the officer was given a clear explanation of what was required, whereupon the proceedings were commenced.

I pitched up at a Magistrates' Court one morning to find a couple of other members of the team also there with an arrest they had made the night before. I should normally have been on nights with them, but had been taken off night duty as I was due at court and I had also been on aid the previous day. I was unaware of events that had taken place, which had been one of our regulars who had gone berserk, resulting in him being arrested and held at the station overnight. Apparently he had decided he wouldn't come out of the cell without a fight and to make matters worse he had covered his cell in excrement.

Big Mac explained to me that Martin had gone into one and asked if I could stand next to him in case he kicked off again. He couldn't as he would have to leave the court prior to the start of the hearing as he was a witness and would have to be out of the court before the case started. Of course I was only too happy to help, I didn't however know about the rest of the story otherwise I would have armed myself with gloves at the very least.

This particular court was nearly always armed with JPs. At my first station after training school the court and the staff were very helpful, but this one was the complete opposite. In fact in my service this was the only court I didn't like to go to. The court rose to acknowledge the JPs enter the courtroom and the first case, Martin's, was called. As the charge was read out Martin decided to ignore the charge and start to call the magistrates and anyone else he could mention a variety of names, none of them particularly pleasant, flattering or polite. It wasn't for me to interrupt Martin so until I was directed otherwise I was quite happy to stand by until directed otherwise by the magistrates.

Eventually enough was enough and I was ordered by the JPs to take Martin back to the cells. Fortunately the dock where he was standing was very close to the exit door. As I took hold of one of his arms and led him to the door he began to resist. Martin was quite a large bloke, certainly bigger than me. I didn't want a violent struggle in the middle of the courtroom, there was far too much furniture and knowing the JPs they would probably be more upset with me than him.

With a big shove I managed to get him through the door and I wasn't surprised as he took a huge punch at me, which I managed to duck. I never took my truncheon with me to court and rarely carried it on patrol, it was very light and useless as I have mentioned, other than for breaking windows. Until anyone else came to my assistance it was just me and him. With a carefully aimed punch I hit Martin hard under the chin, knocking him to the floor. I quickly jumped on top of him to restrain him as court officers began to arrive to assist me. As well as not wanting him to punch my lights out, I didn't fancy him escaping either, as that could cost you some money if a discipline board decided you had not done everything possible to prevent the prisoner from making off.

After the short struggle I returned to the court to explain that Martin had been restrained and was being taken back to his cell. I was thanked by the court who asked what the next case was. As I looked to the back of the court Big Mac was smiling and he nodded his head for me to join him outside, which I did.

He began to laugh and explained the version he had witnessed from his side of the door. Out of view he heard Martin shout to me, 'You fascist bastard!' followed by a thump with a reply from me along the lines of, 'Have that you bastard!' Perhaps I was wrong about our JPs: I never heard another word, I certainly didn't get a complaint, but I still made a record of the events in my pocket book just in case. Of course I thanked Big Mac for the update on the excrement-covered cell and quickly made my way to the toilets to have a good wash and brush up.

One of my old inspectors tells a lovely story about when she worked on a squad and as one of the few female officers she was required to play the innocent young girl in a park, following recent incidents of females being 'flashed' at. On this day she had a guy flash at her and then he began to play with himself. Of course he was arrested and charged with outraging public decency.

A few months later the matter was brought before the Crown Court. My inspector, then a young detective constable, gave her evidence and waited as the defence brief cross-examined her about the incident. In typical style he clarified how far away she was and eventually she was asked, 'How exactly would you describe my client as "playing with himself"?'

Looking to the judge, then the jury, she replied, 'I should imagine you could describe that far better than me, but if I was pushed I would say the same way that you would play with yourself.'

Good girl. The jury thought it was hilarious. The defence barrister obviously didn't, as he retook his seat looking very flushed. I think you could call that game, set and match.

10

The Old Days, Those Were the Ways . . . Weren't They?

Some of my favourite times during my days in the job would be the tales of other coppers in bygone days. These would invariably take place around the canteen as each officer would recount their particular favourite. They never ceased to amaze me, particularly in the earlier days of policing when there was a far stricter regime than I ever experienced, which was enforced by the sergeants and inspectors. Whilst the constables had their 'tea holes', probably visited a few years earlier by the now sergeants, it was very much poacher turned gamekeeper.

One particular old sweat was a real dry old stick. He was a solid old lump, and whenever he spoke his speech was always very slow and deliberate, which made me laugh even more when he recounted some of his old stories. Even now at my age I can still get an attack of the giggles and as a child my mum would demand I stop it because she would be missing other jokes from regular TV shows.

Well, I shall call this old cop 'Bomber'. One particular night duty he had been posted to a walking beat. The rules were quite clear: if you were walking you had to wear boots. If, however, you were posted to a driving duty, you would be allowed to wear shoes. At the same time this incident occurred officers also had to sign into a book, stating the reason for their return to the station. Invariably it would be for a mealbreak, an arrest or a comfort break, because you would undoubtedly be challenged by a supervisory officer.

This particular day Bomber was caught red-handed in the station by the duty inspector, who didn't challenge the fact he was skulking around in the station, but did notice that he was wearing shoes and he had quite clearly been given a walking beat on parade. 'Why are you wearing shoes Bomber? You are posted to a walking beat,' demanded the inspector.

'Oh that's it sir, ask me why I'm wearing shoes,' drawled Bomber. 'Don't ask me if I have got a problem with my feet.'

Taken aback, the inspector apologised and said, 'Well Bomber have you got something wrong with your feet?'

'No sir, but it would be nice if you asked.' And with this Bomber quickly about turned and left before further enquiries were made of him regarding his presence in the station.

In the 'good old days', parades would require officers to produce their 'appointments'. Officers' appointments consisted of a truncheon, pocket book and whistle, which would be examined closely, if the sergeant or inspector felt the need. One particular shift the duty inspector noticed that Bomber was not wearing a watch. He immediately pointed this out to Bomber, who stated that he didn't own a watch and furthermore the regulations didn't require him to. 'Bomber, tomorrow on parade you will bring with you a timepiece. It is imperative that an officer is aware of the exact time for any eventuality.'

The following evening Bomber stood to attention as the parade was taken, whereupon the duty inspector required all officers to produce their timepieces. At the required moment the inspector stood in front of Bomber and asked him to produce his timepiece. Bomber pulled out from under his tunic a small Mickey Mouse alarm clock, which was draped around his neck on a rough piece of string. With this a shout of, 'What do you think you are doing!' could be heard around the station as the inspector tried to calm himself.

'Well sir, if I remember correctly you directed me to have a timepiece. This is a very accurate timepiece and the only one I have.' With this the inspector left one of his sergeants to deal with him.

Around these times every officer was expected to know the rules contained in an instruction book. Each officer was issued with their copy of this at training school, but could choose to return it upon completion of ten years' service. For those officers who chose to take the promotion examinations, they had to apply for a copy of the *General Instructions*. These consisted of a further two large books and covered just about everything you could ever require to know in day-to-day policing. Bomber regularly reminded senior officers that whilst he did his utmost to keep up to date with the instruction book, he couldn't possibly be expected to keep up with a book he had deliberately chosen to avoid for many years, unless of course it suited him, which it occasionally did!

As well as appointments, officers were required to have a number of report books with them. At another parade the senior officer required each and every officer to produce the said books. Bomber proudly held his pocket book out, which received an immediate admonishment for its tardy approach. Such behaviour would not be tolerated in the future and the following day once again he, along with the rest of the team, would be required to have every single item that a patrolling officer could be required to need in the course of their duties, as per the instruction book.

The following shift Bomber stood before the parade with every pocket of his tunic bulging. The inspector demanded to know what the meaning of such an outrage was. Bomber in his usual slow drawl said, 'Well sir, after the error of my ways yesterday I took it upon myself to investigate all that I should need as you directed. I've made a list in case other officers would like to be as professional as me. It consists so far of three accident books, three process books, three incident report books, one HORT/1, the address of the local town hall and Citizens Advice Bureau, vet form 1 in the eventuality I need a vet to put an animal down . . .'

'Enough, enough, enough, enough!' exploded the inspector.

'You have made your point, which you have also chosen to miss!' Exasperated the inspector again left the parade, beaten at his own game, knowing it, but no doubt thinking of the next move.

Bomber seemed to delight in challenging senior officers. On one occasion he explained how the chief superintendent had given him an unfair bollocking. That couldn't be right he said, you should get your facts right. You may have known he had done something wrong, but you needed proof. After all, wasn't that what was expected of him before he affected an arrest? Let's face it, he said, taking away someone's liberty was a serious matter, why did they forget this when they went up the ranks? Something had to be done about it and it was.

A short while later Bomber explained that he had read the chief superintendent's 728. Now, a 728 is a form that requires details of just about any incident, or request from a police officer and invariably is submitted to your boss for their consideration, comments and recommendations. This particular 728 Bomber said started very well: 'Dear sir, I beg to report the loss of my warrant card'. Now this is still taken seriously, but probably even more so at this time.

'Well?' proclaimed Bomber, 'how did I know he kept his warrant card in his tunic?'

'What do you mean?' asked another PC.

'When I threw the chief superintendent's tunic in the boiler, I didn't know he had his warrant card in it. That is an important document and the instruction manual clearly states it should be on your person at all times, in the eventuality that you should deal with something off duty, which as we all know you may be required to do.'

There is no doubt that today, if there was the slightest hint of this sort of behaviour, there would be a full investigation, criminal charges and a criminal record for the officer concerned as well as being sacked from the job.

Despite some of his ways, Bomber was keen to help where he felt the need. On one occasion he was called into a shop, where he was met by the staff who had detained a young lady, who had a few children in tow. Apparently she had attempted to take a pair of shoes for one of her children without paying.

'What's this all about then? Bomber enquired.

After some encouraging the lady explained that her husband had run off and left her with no money. The eldest child, who was just about to start school, needed a new pair of shoes so he wouldn't be a laughing stock.

The tough old cop did no more than put his hand in his pocket, pay for the shoes and send the lady and her children off home with words of advice, including how to get help. When this became local knowledge, much to his annoyance, he tried to deny it, saying that the story had clearly been exaggerated.

Whilst patrolling his beat one bright morning he came across a neighbour dispute. The problem quite simply was one neighbour was parking his large camper van across the drive way of his neighbour and had refused to move it, despite attempts to sort the problem out amicably. Eventually and rather amazingly Bomber was forced to report the man for obstruction of the highway and actually completed the necessary report, which he duly had supervised and submitted to the correct office back at the nick in order that the man could be prosecuted.

A couple of weeks later Bomber was again on patrol outside the offender's home. The man ran up to Bomber, thrusting a letter in his face, which clearly stated that a decision on this occasion had been made to take no further action for the obstruction. Of course he was warned that future offences might not be treated so leniently. To make matters worse the vehicle owner told Bomber that his 'betters' had seen the light. With this Bomber stood back, looked at the nice new camper van and said, 'I should think a fine vehicle of this size would require a two-pump attendance in the unlikely eventuality that it should catch fire.'

'What are you saying, what are you saying? Are you saying you are going to burn my camper van?' the highway obstructer asked.

'Oh no sir, I couldn't possibly threaten to commit a criminal offence. I could end up in all sorts of trouble, but I would suspect that such a fire would leave a big pile of ash. Good day sir, take care.'

Two things happened after this. Firstly, the camper van was correctly positioned, secondly Bomber went to the relevant unit back at the station and told them that the day he needed their help in order to do nothing he would retire – he was more than capable of doing nothing himself, without any assistance.

Regardless of individuals' thoughts on police officers, I have seen a lot of generous acts by fellow officers. Big Mac came back to the station after he had reported a burglary on his beat one morning, the victim an elderly female, who amongst other things had discovered her pension money had been taken. He added up how many officers there were on duty and made a request from each to replace the stolen pension money and help the poor old love out.

One early shift I went to an address where another elderly lady had lost her front door keys and didn't have a spare. When I arrived she was accompanied by her nephew who was not being very helpful. Eventually I had to break the door open to gain entry, which caused some damage, but it wasn't too bad. I have repaired locks for people in the past, or at least managed to cobble something together until a proper job could be done later, but I didn't have the time that day as our control room already had other calls for me. Having an insecure home is never a comforting thought, particularly for an older member of the public.

I didn't want to go until I could sort something out but the nephew was about as useful as the proverbial chocolate teapot and he was telling me that he would have to go soon. I very quickly told him that he would stay where he was for the time being as it was the least anyone could do, particularly a concerned relative. I asked the lady if she had any money for a new lock, which she didn't. Consequently I phoned a local locksmith company who I knew were excellent and explained the circumstances and found the best price they would be able to do the job for. They clearly would not make anything out of the job, if they even covered the cost of the lock. I never carried a lot of money with me when I was on duty but gave what I had to the old lady and got her nephew to part with the rest, then shot off explaining they would be arriving very shortly.

Later that evening, when I got home, I explained to my mum over the family dinner how infuriating this nephew had been and that a good shake might have woken him up a bit. I explained how I gave some money towards the cost and she said, 'Thank God for that, I thought you were becoming a right hard case, it's nice to know my son is still in there somewhere.' I was still very young in service but I found myself at one of those steep learning curves again. Good old mum.

One of the most disgusting stories I heard was told to me by JD when I was a probationer. It related to his RAF days and another guy who was also in the job. Apparently he and JD didn't see eye to eye. Some years later I heard the same story but from the other officer.

JD explained how as a young man he had gone out one particular evening and ended up with a young lady and 'did the dirty deed'. As he was making his way back to his barracks he began to think about the consequences of his actions. What if she had some disease? If she was quick to jump into bed with him, how many other people had she jumped into bed with?

Back at the barracks and a little worse for wear he decided to clean certain parts of his anatomy with a toothbrush, but not just any toothbrush, so he chose one belonging to a colleague known as 'Posh Paws'. After making a thorough job of it he returned the toothbrush and crashed out into his pit. He intended by all accounts to make good with the toothbrush later in the morning, but he awoke late and found that Posh Paws had already made good use of his cleaning item. Nonetheless JD decided he had to tell one of his mates, who told someone else, and eventually Posh Paws got to hear about it and clearly he wasn't best pleased as you can expect, and a disagreement understandably was had.

Posh was telling this story about ten years later. I couldn't admit

I knew the culprit, but to be fair to JD and Posh both versions were very similar. JD's version ended in a great guffaw, whilst Posh's version ended in 'dirty rotten bastard'.

An incident I witnessed in a pub after we had policed Prince Charles marrying Lady Diana Spencer probably best shows one of the biggest differences between police officers then and now.

We had been up since about two in the morning in order to be ground assigned several hours before the royal couple even appeared. When we got back to our station, everyone was tired but fancied a pint. It was unanimously decided that we should go to our local where we began to enjoy ourselves after such a long day and being part of such an auspicious occasion; why, we had witnessed history.

Our inspector for the day liked a drink and he had sunk more than enough by this time. He obviously thought it was time to liven the evening up, so he declared to a few of us standing nearby, 'See that long-legged attractive woman standing near the pool table over there?' He indicated a very attractive lady in her late twenties. We all nodded our heads before he went on. 'I'm going to go over there and I'm going to grab her bum see, she's then going to turn round you see, take one look at me and slap me across the face. I'll roll over the pool table still holding my pint see, and then I'll signal everything is OK by raising my glass, all right?'

Before anyone could suggest it wouldn't be a good idea, if they even thought it wasn't a good idea, he was gone. Sure enough he grabbed the young lady by her buttocks, and she turned around and delivered him the most fantastic slap across the face. Exactly as he stated he did a lovely roll across the pool table and still managed to keep hold of his pint, despite his condition. He looked across to us and shouted, 'You see, I told you!'

Today I cannot begin to think of the amount of aggravation this sort of incident would cause. The pub would no doubt have emptied very quickly, at least of coppers, with thoughts of allegations of a sexual assault and all the trouble that would undoubtedly follow.

At one station where I worked we had an officer who was called 'Posh Eric'. This would become obvious very quickly to anyone who met him. Eric was a good London boy, with an obvious London accent. Rather than dropping his aitches he emphasised them or added them where he thought it appropriate, not too dissimilar to Parker out of *Thunderbirds*, but every now and again he would revert to type.

He told an amusing story one day, which was soon to be made an offence by the Communications Act.

'H'ive got this bloody dog near me h'and the h'owner keeps letting it shit h'everywhere. H'i had given him a number h'of warnings h'of the consequences the next time h'it shat in my garden, which h'in fact was last week. So I scooped h'it h'up h'and put it h'in h'an h'envelope h'and posted it frew h'his door. H'it would appear to 'ave solved the problem.'

11

Driving

I mentioned earlier that the driving school is at Hendon. After getting through your initial training, you began to get aspirations of what it would be like to drive a police car. Today you can drive a police car without doing any course, in order to attend minor calls, but you are prevented from exceeding the speed limit, or using a blue light to get to a call. In my day the best you could hope for would be the occasional passenger seat and some respite from walking. If you proved yourself worthy you would be allowed to attend the first of three possible courses, comprising the driving of pandas, vans and ultimately the area car.

To drive the pandas you had to complete a three-week course, now known as the Response Course. Later you would be shown the correct way to drive the van, which concentrated on reversing and towing correctly. Finally, if you were deemed worthy, you would be allowed to attend the Area Car Course, which would be completed in two stages. The first part was four weeks at the driving school. If you were still deemed worthy you would be allowed back to your station, where you would be partnered with an experienced area car driver before returning to complete the final two weeks. At the end, if you passed, you would have a final drive and if you passed this would result in you being awarded a Class I or Class II, the difference between the two only a couple of marks.

Standards at the driving school were extremely high. Before you were even allowed near a car you had to pass an eyesight test and a written examination on the Highway Code and Road Craft, which explained how every police driver should drive correctly, and should assist you to avoid accidents, or at least reduce the risk of them being your fault. You just had to follow the 'system'.

Every parade would require all students to wear their flat caps, which you could wear in replacement of the better-known beat duty hat when posted to driving duty. Tunics and trousers would be required with sharp creases, or the instructors could send you back to your Division. Occasionally even the senior officer in charge of the driving school would attend. He had a fearsome reputation, they all seemed to. If they had had Facebook in those days they would have made terrifying reading.

When I did my Response Course we had the good fortune to experience the skidpan. I had been sent on the course with Darrell, who was still reunited with his truncheon. The instructor gave us a run through the procedure as he accelerated at a frightening speed towards the skidpan, with a barrier not far the other side of it, followed by a walkway and a drop. As we hit the skidpan the car began to slide and with an experienced hand at the wheel the instructor began to apply the brakes in what he described as 'cadence braking'. This is what the modern car fitted with an anti-locking braking system, or ABS, does, but ABS does it even more efficiently. We were taught to hit the brake very quickly, remove your foot and continue to do this in a machine-gun type effect until you had the car under control and navigated around any obstacle. With considerable ease the instructor steered us around the skidpan and neatly exited and drove back to the starting point.

'You see,' he said, 'that's all there is to it, who wants to go first?'

With some further explanation and some recapping, we took it in turns. I did OK as did the other student, which only left Darrell. Now, it is important at all times to follow the advice of the instructor. At some point, I would estimate in this case at the point of Darrell applying the brakes, he had a change of heart – this is not good. Cadence braking when needed is needed immediately, it is a one-off opportunity, and time is of the essence. There was no doubt we were skidding most fantastically, in fact we seemed to be picking up speed. Even the shouts of the instructor couldn't bring Darrell back from the brink as he kept his foot locked down on the brake, before we were slammed into the bank. Fortunately Darrell had followed the other important piece of advice and entered the skidpan at a far lower speed than the instructor.

Oh dear.

After several attempts we all got the hang of it and we all went on to pass the course.

On one course a foolhardy student decided he would put the senior officer's sense of humour to the test. Didn't he go through Hendon? They have their sense of humour removed upon arrival, and it's a requirement of the job. Standing to attention and looking immaculate, the officer, who was halfway through his Area Car Course, had correctly worked out the day the senior officer would attend the parade. As the boss walked down the line he made a few comments to officers on miniscule corrections they should make for the next parade, or else. As he arrived at our wag his attention was drawn to a small piece of cotton that was on his tunic lapel. This wouldn't do, so he pulled the cotton off and pulled and pulled as the cotton reel, secreted in the wag's trouser pocket, continued to unfold. No we can confirm, definitely no sense of humour, as another familiar explosion took place, with the officer being directed back to his station, no doubt kicking himself after all his hard work.

Oh very dear.

After you complete your driving course you cannot wait to get back to your station to be given the ultimate power of responding to calls on your own. The whole world would be your oyster; well, if the more experienced members of the team didn't have anything to say about it.

I was eating my breakfast one morning. I had passed my driving course some months earlier when the radio announced that a man was going berserk with an axe. Like every other officer I ran to my police car and met one of my sergeants, known affectionately as

Geordie. The inside of Geordie's hat always made me smile. He had a number of station codes written inside with lines drawn through them, finally finishing with a question mark. This all just about fitted on the band on the inside of his hat. Officers who arrived on the scene began to call for urgent assistance. This meant you would still drive to the system, but you would attempt to pull out all the stops.

After a few miles going as fast as I could I found myself at the road where the call was, but I was still a few hundred yards away when a refuse truck began to reverse across the road towards us. I immediately changed down a gear and accelerated hard through the gap and shortly after I screeched to a halt outside the address, to see the man had just been arrested and the message being relayed on the radio for all units too cancel. The sergeant got out and checked that everything was being done before he started to walk to another police car.

'Come on then Sarge,' I called, 'we can go back and finish our breakfast now.'

In his strong accent he replied, 'I'm not going anywhere with you, you're fu**ing mad. As for my breakfast I doubt I will be able to keep f**k all down for days.' He flatly refused to come with me and furthermore he didn't finish his breakfast. To make matters worse, when we bumped into our duty inspector he told him I was mad as well.

'Sarge, I am not mad. I went there as fast as this car could take us. At no time was I out of my braking distance or putting us or the public in any danger.'

'What do you think that fu**ing big rubbish truck was then, you fu**ing maniac.'

I think he may have eaten a bad egg.

There are dangers attached to driving police cars and I don't just mean the dangers of travelling at high speed. In the eventuality of an accident, regardless of how minor, you would have to reckon with the garage sergeant. Once again the rules are somewhat different in our modern policing world. In my early days you would have to face the quizzing of some gnarled old professional who would have reported just about every kind of accident known to man, heard just about every excuse invented. If the members of the public thought the average cop could be a menace at times like these, this was nothing compared to the poor officer generally totally outmatched against the garage sergeant.

The garage sergeant is a traffic officer who covers quite a number of police Divisions, invariably with a large number of years under his or her belt. As soon as they pulled up you could see suspicion written on their faces and with good reason, it has to be said, because police officers don't like to admit that something was as a result of their poor driving. You might be able to take the mickey about the lack of the size of certain body parts, way before you could criticise a police officer's driving ability. Of course, the garage sergeant became gnarled and crusty through years of excuses and these would include, amongst other things, a dog that ran in front of the vehicle and had to be avoided at all costs. Such was the success of this manoeuvre that the dog had in fact escaped completely unharmed for a number of years, but despite this ageing dog it never showed signs of any grey according to police witnesses. Another fact that would be interesting would be the lack of members of the public shouting, 'He did ever so well to avoid that dog, he deserves a medal.'

Some years ago, I sat, bored, doing my station office duty when the teleprinter chirped into action. It was my responsibility to check all such messages during my tour of duty and initiate any necessary responses. Invariably this meant giving it the next message number before adding it to the pile for the day on a message pad.

That night shift I read the message, which declared that the long-missing black dog, which had been responsible for numerous police accidents had finally met its match with an area car. Whilst it was sad to see the end of this long relationship between the Met and our favoured black dog, it had finally met an untimely end, namely the front end of a Rover SD1. Therefore it would no longer be acceptable to provide any future garage sergeants with the 'black dog' explanation any longer. Sorry dog lovers.

Unfortunately I have had a few meetings with garage sergeants. On one such occasion a panda was being driven by a female officer who began to negotiate a long curving bend at a steady 30mph, when a car reversed off a driveway, causing Carol to brake hard in order to avoid an accident. As she did this the ratchet on the driver seat of the panda gave way and Carol lost her grip on the steering wheel as she was thrown onto her back. The police car hit the kerb before coming to a stop. I attended to commence the accident report, which I had completed, when enter the garage sergeant.

It was customary when you have been responsible for an accident to take the good garage sergeant back to your station and ensure that they were treated to a milky coffee. This particular sergeant was not in a good mood from the off. There may have been many reasons for this, we all have bad ones. Having heard the explanation of events he began to patrol the length of the kerb. The offending car, oblivious to events, had long since disappeared, not helping Carol's cause much at all. Extending his search he returned to the panda and declared that there were no marks to be seen anywhere on the kerb and clearly the accident had occurred elsewhere. There was nothing else for it, all the details would have to be completed back at the station. With this I explained that I had other calls to attend to and offered him the accident book.

'There's no point giving me that mate, it will only reflect the pack of lies I have heard so far, you can come back with us.'

At this stage Carol was becoming upset, because I had asked if the events were accurate as soon as I arrived, which she assured me they were long before the arrival of our garage skipper. In an effort to assist, Carol said to the traffic officer, 'Shall I drive the panda back Sarge?'

'I don't think so young lady, you have done more than enough damage.' (The damage being in fact a very small dent on the wheel rim.) 'No, I shall drive this back and my officer here will follow me to the nick in my car.'

With this he jumped into the panda and went to accelerate away, clearly intending it to be a rather swift getaway. As he did this the ratchet gave way on the seat for the second time and the car lurched to a halt, leaving the sergeant sprawled out headlong in the driver seat. As it was a hot day I threw my report book through the open window and told the sergeant that he might need it. He didn't get a milky coffee.

One story I was told about involved a police vehicle, which had killed the first known badger for some considerable years in Central London. So newsworthy was this that a number of interested groups set about to investigate, as these were indeed interesting times if the badger was returning after such a long absence. The garage sergeant, suspecting (not without good cause) some foul play had to agree that the animal was the correct size for the damage caused. What apparently happened was all correct, but at a different location. The driver had in fact gone off his ground for an errand of mercy. Now whilst this was not too far, you can't admit to a supervisor that you were off your ground, or there would be consequences. None of us ever liked consequences, they were always messy things. The poor animal was dead as a result of it going straight into the path of the police car – nothing was going to change that, the operator was told. The easiest thing was simply to relocate it and save all that paperwork. 'There you go,' said the driver, 'I'll be saving the job loads of paperwork.' Job done.

One night duty I had dealt with a 'fail to stop' accident, which had involved an off-duty police officer. I quickly dealt with the necessary paperwork at the scene before returning to the station to make some follow-up enquiries. As I sat in the panda in the police yard, about to top and tail my report, I suddenly remembered something I needed to do immediately. Wasting no further time, I jumped out of the car and ran over to the back door. As I entered the code on the keypad I heard a faint noise behind me and as I looked around I noticed that I had parked the panda on the only rise in the yard, which my car was now reversing down and heading for the only other car in the yard, parked directly in its path. I wasn't a bad runner in those days, but the inevitable was about to happen. CRUNCH. I did comment on this immediately. It went something like, s**t, f**k, f**t, bo**ocks and so on, I think you get what I mean.

I now had that horrible stomach-clenching moment again. I had about four years' service and I thought I had managed to lose that feeling, clearly I was mistaken. I moved the panda back to a sensible position and began to think of cunning stories that would convince the garage sergeant that it could not possibly have been my fault and if I was really lucky they might even recommend me to be pushed forward to undertake the Area Car Course.

What to do? What to do? What to do? Right, action was required. Let me test the handbrake, there may be a little give, but it was every officer's responsibility to check their vehicle *before* taking a police car out on the road. In the eventuality that something went wrong you had to return to the station and complete a form 54, which stated the defect, which would be rectified as soon as possible, before the car was allowed to be used again. Steadying myself I pulled on the handbrake, click, and click, and there we go, just about another click. Ah, this wasn't looking good, this was probably the best handbrake in the entire fleet of Met vehicles, let alone my station. I had it: I needed to make the handbrake appear as if it may have slipped, and I had a cunning plan forming in my mind. There was nothing else for it so I began to pull the handbrake up for a good five minutes, with a fair amount of violence. Let's check it now I thought, that must have had some effect, and sweat was pouring off my forehead. Click, click, and just about click. Oh f**k, there was nothing else for it, the early hours of Monday morning and at the end of a week of night duty, with a quick change over (in this case a quick change over meant you finished duty at 6 a.m. and had to be back eight hours later, including travelling, washing, shaving and if possible some food) facing me and I had to go and crunch the bloody car.

Whilst I waited for the garage sergeant I completed all my other tasks before about 5 a.m. when he appeared. I had seen him around the stations before and he had a reputation for being fair. I couldn't ask for any more than that. At this point I decided to explain *exactly* how the accident had happened, although my attempt on the handbrake may have been overlooked. I didn't want to cloud his judgement of me.

With this the sergeant let out a big gasp, looked me straight in the eye and said, 'I've been a garage sergeant for over twenty years. In all that time I have done numerous night duties. This week I was within one hour for the first time ever of going a whole week without dealing with a single police accident (POLACC), until you.' (Oh dear.) 'If you hadn't told me the truth I would have removed your testicles, put them in your exhaust, accelerated hard and made sure that you would never have had any chance to darken this good earth with any of your offspring. As it is I shall give you three points, let's hope we don't meet again.' And away he went.

'That didn't go too badly did it,' I said to my sergeant, once the garage sergeant was well out of earshot. My police driving record showed the accident was to count against my driving record, which at least meant there was no immediate chance of being taken off driving duty and whilst I didn't get a recommendation to go on the Area Car Course I was still mobile. Happy days, my testicles were also still intact.

I have been fortunate that I have never been suspended from driving. In the event of a serious accident involving a police car or when the garage sergeant considers a police officer was driving well below the expected standard, they can suspend the officer immediately from driving, and believe me this does happen.

*

On one very busy late turn as a sergeant, the team were short so I took the van out. Within the space of about forty minutes I had been given three home address searches, details of a prisoner that needed to be collected from another police station and, by the way, what time could I relieve the custody officer? Was I the only person on duty? I was mumbling to myself as I reversed into the yard to get the details relating to the house searches. In between mumbling and moaning I scraped the back of the van against the wall. Oh great. A quick inspection revealed that the scuff mark was there to stay and I had no option but to call it in and I requested the garage sergeant. F**k it, I would have to take the van off the road and I would have to spend the rest of the shift in custody, and while we're about it, f**k the home address searches as well.

Within a very short space of time a traffic motorcycle pulled into the police yard, but it wasn't a garage sergeant, it was a garage inspector. Oh bloody deep joy. The inspector asked me what had happened so I explained it all exactly, ending with, 'Sir, this is an example of absolutely appalling driving on my part, it only leaves you to suspend me from driving, which is the very least I deserve.'

'You're being far too hard on yourself sergeant, I have checked the log book for the vehicle against all the old accidents and clearly this is old damage, so you can get straight back to all those jobs you were telling me about.' I didn't bloody believe it, the only time I would (and indeed did) want to get pulled from driving I was back in the driving seat in record time: no bollocking, no points on my police driving record and already my radio was going for me to do other jobs; just how long did they think these jobs took? Moan, groan, moan, and groan, as I left the yard.

On one of my rare sorties as a probationer in a police vehicle I found myself with Posh Roy. He had a few errands to run and I would be of some use if there was any need for an arrest or general writing duty. I didn't mind, it was a break from walking and I needed all the experience I could get.

For some reason he decided to go off road. I can't even remember the reason why now, but as we drove over this muddy track the inevitable happened and we found we were truly stuck. The driving school doesn't teach you how to get out of this situation, because you shouldn't have got into it in the first place. More revving failed to release us and in fact our wheels had buried a good distance, when all of a sudden on the horizon appeared a Land Rover. Not any Land Rover, one equipped with all the necessary equipment to tow old sweats out of the mud, which this kind gentleman did. As we drove off Roy said to me, 'This will just stay between the two of us you realise.' I couldn't help myself, I was young and impetuous, so I told JD. What I didn't realise was that Roy and JD were not the best of buddies so the story was very quickly doing the rounds. The next day as I passed Roy he gave me a contemptuous look, stared me in the eye and said, 'Bastard,' and walked off. Oh dear, I suppose I deserved that.

As well as experiencing the thrill of off-road events I found that not all drivers followed the system they taught you at Hendon. 'Fruit', for instance, when he drove the van would be seen with his beat helmet on and his Sherlock Holmes-type pipe stuck out of the side of his mouth. At times I wondered if I wasn't living through some sort of Will Hay film.

12

Custody and Prisoners

A charge room is generally a hive of activity, with prisoners waiting to be booked in, charged or bailed. Sergeants are busy trying to manage which prisoner needs to come out for interview or talk with a solicitor on a phone, as well as chasing up investigating officers. I spent a number of years as a sergeant managing busy custody suites and it is a busy job.

As a probationer I was watching a sergeant book a prisoner in. As he did this the door opened and I moved out the way to let Big Karl in. As the prisoner was asked his name and address he began to become aggressive and I was quite surprised that the sergeant didn't order him to be searched and placed in a cell until he behaved himself.

Again he was asked for his details and again the sergeant was met with an aggressive reply, when Karl very gently tapped him on the shoulder. With this the prisoner turned around violently, no doubt expecting me to still be standing there, only to find I had in fact been replaced by Karl. Karl, despite being a very large man, spoke very quietly, and simply said, 'My sergeant has asked you a very simple question, very politely. Now if you and I are to get on I suggest you turn around like a good boy and very politely answer the nice sergeant's questions.' With a nod of his head the prisoner turned around very quickly and began to provide all the details (very wisely) far quicker than the sergeant could write. Karl had that effect on people.

I got told off during my probation by another one of the nice sergeants on my relief. I had been called to an estate with an engine revving at maximum revs. We didn't need an exact location, we just followed the noise of the screeching engine. When we arrived we found that a young lad who had been out celebrating and couldn't get back into his flat had decided to put his car engine on for some warmth. Unfortunately he fell asleep and at some point his leg landed on the accelerator, waking the entire estate who eventually called us. I had to arrest him, once I had managed to wake him up for being drunk in charge of the motor vehicle.

Once back at the station a divisional surgeon was called and she conducted a number of tests to ascertain if he was drunk in charge. At one point the poor sod was asked a number of mental arithmetic questions, which he was getting badly wrong. I had to walk away because I was starting to get the giggles, something that hadn't gone unnoticed by the sergeant who discussed this with me once the doctor had left.

'Sarge I'm very sorry, I didn't mean to be disrespectful but I doubt if the guy could have answered those questions if he had been stone cold sober, I don't think the doctor realised that.'

I was given a serious bollocking and told in future if I had any cause for such thoughts I should mention them discreetly to the sergeant at the time.

When I was posted to another station after completing my probationary period, I met a sergeant who had been sent back to team for his last eighteen months' service. Brian found nights quite difficult at this time and one night was found by the duty inspector who had been looking for him. As there were no prisoners Brian decided he should make the most of it, so he took his shoes off, got a blanket and went to sleep on the divisional surgeon's examination table. He thought it was quite acceptable as he was on duty, ready to deal with anything that came through the charge room door, except the inspector. Oh how times have changed.

As a custody sergeant on a few rare occasions I found that I had a quiet moment in custody. Once even, at the start of a Saturday night duty, I took over, bailed my one and only prisoner and felt quite pleased with myself, when a fellow sergeant paid me a visit, to be disgusted that I wasn't busy and clearly I wouldn't need a break to get a sandwich later. I explained to him. 'Tony, when you have a grasp of the custody suite as I have here and you keep on top of all your duties you will be rewarded with a nice clear custody suite. You could learn a thing or two.' Tony had been a sergeant a lot longer than I had and he had showed me a number of things around the custody suite when I first arrived.

He left, saying that he was going to do his damndest to go and arrest a coachload of hooligans. After I dealt with the mundane responsibilities of checking the property, I meandered to the control room with a cup of tea to see what was happening beyond the walls of the nick. As I did this, Lou, a very nice lady who worked in our control room, updated me that there had been a nasty assault at one of our local pubs. This call was quickly updated with details of the suspect making off in a fifty-two-seater coach. This can't be happening, I thought. I had no doubt who would be attending and whilst I do not have any gifts of mediumship I knew what was going to happen and I wasn't wrong. To make matters worse, the coach was full. It got worse still: the female victim was unconscious and the reporting officers couldn't identify if the suspect was male or female. This was beginning to be a very bad dream.

Tony looked pleased with himself when he came into the charge room and provided me with the facts of the case. I had fifty-two people waiting in the back yard to be booked in. I established that we had an officer with the victim and directed that they be spoken to immediately to reduce the number of people to book in by half if we could at least identify the gender of the suspect. In the end all of them were booked in. I only had fourteen cells, but fortunately, with the assistance of two other sergeants and the duty officer, we waded our way through it all. In those days you sometimes had three to a cell, but it was rare. Today it is one person per cell.

As Tony went off to complete his notes he mentioned that he

couldn't relieve me for grub as he was involved in the case, but of course I had his utmost sympathy. He didn't look too upset. When we discovered the gender of the suspect we started to reduce our suspects and then we began to play that board game – did the suspect have hair, glasses, marks or scars? – which still left all the cells full by the time I left at six in the morning, very mentally knackered. I had spoken too soon once again. Would I ever learn? Oh dear.

Amongst many of the regulations every prisoner has to be checked regularly as per Code C of the Codes of Practice. Code C explains everything you need to know when dealing with a prisoner whilst they are in the custody suite. On one such occasion, but not the only time, I spoke to a violent prisoner who shouted at me, 'Who's doing your missus while you're on night duty?'

'Oh I should imagine it's the same bloke who is doing yours, right now, and no doubt making a far better job of it than you do.' It never ceases to amaze me that a grown man can get so upset by something like this, but I clearly hit a raw nerve, as he began to shoulder-barge the cell door repeatedly. I should imagine the bruises were with him for some days after.

The custody sergeant also has to check to see if a prisoner has anything on them that they could use to harm themselves while in custody. Unfortunately it is not unusual for a prisoner to be able to hide a sharp object; even when a thorough search has been conducted, the search can only go so far (unless you get authority from a senior officer), as I know from personal experience.

I was in the charge room on a particular night duty when a violent drunk was being booked in and was requested to empty his pockets. Sure enough he reverted to some sort of Kevin-type character: 'You can't be serious!' and he began to take off all his clothes. Also present was Julie, a lovely young West Country lass. As the prisoner stood before everyone present like the day he was born, he asked the sergeant if he was happy now. Before the sergeant could reply, Julie said, 'Oh, I've heard about those,' looking towards the man's groin, 'but I had been told that they were bigger than that.' With her accent it made it even more hilarious and all except the prisoner roared with laughter as he began to dress himself again, very quickly.

Parents can be quite surprising at times of attending the station to look after their little angels. I led one mum through to the custody suite explaining that little Johnny had decided to spit all over his cell and just so she was aware I had no intention of moving him as I had no doubt he would continue doing the same if I did move him, which would require two cells to be cleaned later instead of one, and I would add some charges for damaging the cell.

The rules require the young person to be reminded of their rights in the presence of an adult so that a decision can be made as to whether they wish a solicitor and also for the sergeant to explain what the arrest was for and why they needed to remain in custody. On this occasion little Johnny was brought out of his cell and his mum simply asked him if he had been spitting in the cell, which he at least admitted. With no further ado she slapped him hard across the face saying that she despised people who spat and ordered him to apologise to me, which he did, still in shock. It wasn't the first time I have had to stop a parent from dealing with their offspring rather robustly.

People under the age of 18 are not generally placed in a cell but a detention room. Apart from a slightly different door I could never work out the real difference – it's still pretty bleak. As I entered the charge room one day to relieve the custody sergeant for his mealbreak I saw this skinny little 13-year-old standing in the centre of the charge room, fists clenched out to his sides shouting, 'It will take a load of you to get me in a cell!' He had not realised I was behind him and I picked him up under one arm and asked the custody sergeant if he had been searched. I was informed that he had been and so placed him in the detention room. Young lads don't like being embarrassed and his entire audience had now broken out into laughter as I carried him very easily, all five stone dripping wet, and informed him it wasn't a cell, but a detention room as he shook his legs in a futile bid to escape.

Another night I found myself doing custody when a lot of officers suddenly found the need to be in the charge room. I soon found the reason why when a young lady was brought in having provided a positive breath test at the scene of an accident. It is a requirement for officers attending accidents to require all drivers to provide a breath test.

I could see why I was so popular all of a sudden: our young lady, in her mid-twenties, was a very attractive brunette, with a stunning figure. I was able to establish how she kept herself so fit, when she informed me that her occupation was an aerobic instructor. I couldn't stand all the drooling so I told all the officers to go back on patrol and make themselves busy, which required leaving the charge room immediately so that those who were already busy, namely me, could get on with matters.

The breath machine at the station, known as an evidential breath machine (EBM) quickly informed me that the young lady was over the limit. She blew between 40 and 50 on the machine, which simply meant she could choose to replace this sample by providing a sample of blood. 'I can't do that, I am anaemic,' she told me. Well I know my first aid had never been that good but surely this was a no brainer. Still, I couldn't attend court and say 'in my expert opinion', I couldn't have one in such matters, so I called the FME.

When our FME arrived she informed me that a doctor would take more blood to test for anaemia than for our procedure, so the young lady was talking complete nonsense. Despite this she still refused to provide blood and so I charged her with the offence despite the pleas of a young constable clearly very much in lust. I had to get him out of this condition so he was given the opportunity to make his nice sergeant a cup of tea.

*

You get to meet all sorts of prisoners over the years: the hard nut, the smooth talker, the likeable rogue. Some are extremely intelligent and some just think they are. One day I had booked a prisoner in, who like many of his fellow inmates had a number of tattoos. One read something like 'FS and AB forever'. It was quite a neat tattoo, at least it wasn't a home-made job. I listened to the details of the arrest and took all his personal details. His names did not include any initials beginning with F or S, but I assured him that we of course would do our utmost to get him on his way as quickly as possible.

In a nice modern custody suite a quick spin on the modern fingerprint machine, known as NSPIS, would have identified him very quickly. At that moment in time we had to do it a slightly harder way, but it could be more fun. Of course when we did identify him we found him to be an escaper from prison. You can't blame him for trying, it's all part of the game. But remember the old lag's saying: 'If you can't do the time, don't do the crime'.

I upset one defence solicitor late one evening after I refused her client bail. As the prisoner was being taken to his cell she said to me in a sharp tone, 'I don't suppose you have ever sided with a defence brief have you?' She seemed quite annoyed, but I had followed the rules.

I upset her further when I replied, 'Actually I did once, but I later realised I had made a mistake.' It's nothing personal, we are on different sides.

Sergeants are even able to upset their fellow sergeants. Tony, who I mentioned earlier, used to enjoy arresting drunks regardless of the available options and one night he did this with John, who asked him why he felt the need to do this. Did he enjoy making life difficult for his fellow sergeants? At this time most drunks would receive a caution and be released in the morning. On this occasion John decided that Tony needed to be taught a lesson, so an hour before the end of our shift he charged the drunk and then directed Tony to complete all the necessary paperwork.

'But why didn't you caution him?' Tony asked.

'Well I thought, Tony knows how busy it gets in here and he wouldn't arrest a drunk just for the sake of it, just to annoy me, so I thought if it must be serious enough for him to be arrested, he must therefore want me to charge him.'

'But that means I've got to get the papers all done and I've only got an hour before the end of the shift, the boss isn't going to authorise me overtime for that.'

Indeed he was correct. As he went he could be heard moaning about the administrative burden he was faced with. John said, 'Let's see if that changes his ways.'

Another night duty one of my PCs, 'Badger', came into the custody suite with a big smile on his face, followed by a drunk female and her four children aged 6 years and younger. It is an offence to be drunk in charge of a child under 7 and the officer had made the arrest. As he gave the evidence leading up to the arrest he kept getting a small smile on his face. I worked out very quickly that he thought I would be looking after the four young children. He thought wrong.

Finally, when the booking-in procedure had been completed, I let Badger get to the door ready to escape from the custody suite and simply asked, 'Where are you going then Badger?'

'I'm going to the writing room to do my notes for the arrest sarge.'

'That's very good of you Badger, but you're going the wrong way. You can take mum in to the surgeon's room with her four children. You can see they are all getting upset at the prospect of mum being taken away and we wouldn't want that. While you are looking after them, making the children happy with your carefree disposition and playing happy families, you can complete the necessary forms for all the children as well.'

'But Sarge, I've got to do my notes.' The smile now disappeared off his face and his evening had just taken an unexpected turn for the worst.

'Of course you have to do your notes Badger, I understand that, but look on this as one of life's little experiences. You will be able to get an idea of parenthood and how to get on with life while you have upset children around you and yet still complete your notes all at the same time. Won't that be fun?'

A few hours later after the social services had been consulted and the woman declared fit, Badger was released from his nightmare. I asked him, 'Well Badger, have you learnt anything from this?'

'What do you mean Sarge?'

'Well I would have thought that you would have learnt a few things from this episode. One: don't try to have the old custody sergeant over; two: get the children taken to a trusty family member and save lots of unnecessary writing; and three: plan your wind-ups a bit better next time. Remember life is a bit like chess, you have to think of the moves the other player might make as well.'

Looking thoroughly cheesed off, Badger left the custody suite looking a very downhearted chap, mumbling about a number of things, including me and parenthood.

Oh dear.

Following the Brixton riots it was deemed by Lord Scarman that police charge rooms should be visited by lay visitors. These are generally well-meaning people who would arrive unannounced at a charge room and then visit those prisoners who agreed to see them. I experienced this on a large number of occasions. Generally I found them OK. On one visit I was challenged as to why a prisoner was out of his cell mopping and sweeping the floor. The prisoner had been an overstayer in the country and was being deported.

The regulations at the time allowed the Immigration Service to detain prisoners up to five days while they arranged for a flight or detention elsewhere in their own facilities. The rules also stated at the time that they should be offered daily exercise. This could never be achieved for a number of reasons. I explained that the prisoner had been bored and had offered to clean the place up, as it allowed him a bit of time out of the cell. He had done the same job the day before and he had made a very good job of cleaning the cells. He agreed with this when he was asked by the lay visitor. I explained it was the nearest he was going to get to exercise and it did assist his well-being whilst he waited to be returned home. At the end of their visit the lay visitors completed a short report to the chief superintendent and some of them would allow you to see the report, although they were not obliged to. On this occasion I got a glowing report for being open minded to the needs of the prisoners.

I had another visit one blistering summer. I had been posted as a permanent custody officer at this time, not something that I wanted, but you have to get on with it, don't you? As usual the lay visitors made their visits and discussed some of the issues the prisoners had brought to their attention. Not surprisingly all the prisoners had complained about the stifling heat and I was asked if there was anything I could do about it.

I simply stated that the design of a custody suite is such that windows do not open and whilst I agreed the prisoners were staying in intolerable conditions they generally only had to stay for a short period, whereas I and my colleagues who had been sentenced by our senior management to a year of the same also found the conditions intolerable. 'Oh we hadn't thought of that sergeant, that is a very good point.' Off they went to make their report, which they sealed. It turned out that they acknowledged that the conditions were intolerable and recognised how professional the sergeants were, having to also put up with such a difficult environment.

If I had completed a report asking for air conditioning a docket would have been started. It would have gone to one of my bosses, they would have sent it to the relevant departments as its long journey around the Metropolitan Police would have started, the docket increasing in size with the likelihood that no action would ever have been taken. This wasn't the case with our lay visitors, they were like a dog with a bone, they persisted with the case and sure enough the situation was remedied. Well done the lay visitors, who said all those unkind things about Lord Scarman? Shame on you!

We didn't always agree though. One night a young lad had been placed in a cell having flooded his detention room and another cell earlier. When I started duty I was informed of this and the toilet paper had been removed from his cell as well as most of his clothing and blankets to save a further repeat.

I was told by the lay visitors that this was intolerable, which I agreed with. I explained that this was now the third cell he had soiled, which other prisoners would be forced to use, all because of the selfish behaviour of one individual. I refused to move him to another cell, which we were beginning to run out of. Besides, if that was the environment he chose to live in who was I to argue? My colleague Graham didn't give them such high marks for their report this time.

Oh dear.

It must be the environment, because I have had disagreements with officers from my own station in custody, officers from other forces, defence solicitors and social workers. It is impossible to please everyone, it cannot always be done. I charged a six-foot two traveller one night who had informed the earlier custody sergeant that he was 16. He looked similar to Desperate Dan, but the rules state that until you can prove otherwise you have to treat a prisoner accordingly, so he was being treated as a juvenile.

I charged the young lad with 'burglary artifice'. He had managed to hoodwink an elderly lady who lived on her own, allowing him in to her flat, where he kindly helped himself to her belongings. Victims of this offence are generally elderly and are often left very shaken by the experience. At a time when they are most vulnerable they have to look out for this kind of behaviour. This to me is an absolutely unforgiveable crime and people that carry out such crimes are one of the lowest forms of life.

The investigating officer made representations to me that the prisoner should be kept in custody as we had failed to confirm his identity and we didn't believe the details he had provided, which were still being investigated. Also present was his defence solicitor and the local social worker who I had had dealings with in the past. I asked the defence solicitor if they had any comments, which they did, but were very weak, so with this I made my decision that he would remain in custody to appear before the local court at the next hearing.

With this the social worker began to give me a lecture, which I brought to a very quick end. This was the part I had been dreading because the rules meant I had to ask the local authority if they had any suitable accommodation to house our burglar for the night. If they did he would undoubtedly escape and be on the run until a later arrest and identification by fingerprints, assuming the next event didn't follow the same route as this was taking, and how many other victims would there be in the meantime? The social worker was back on her hobby horse. 'You know we don't have any accommodation, that is why you are keeping him in custody, I think this is absolutely despicable, he is only sixteen and shouldn't be kept in here.'

I'd had enough. I confirmed that she couldn't provide any accommodation and told her that the grounds for refusing him bail were quite simple. As far as I was concerned I was there to protect the victim, in this case a very elderly lady, who would rest easier in her bed once she had been informed that our lying *16-year-old* was locked up and furthermore I made no apology for it. The rules stated I had to treat him as a 16-year-old and I would. If she didn't like it I didn't care, and if she wished to complain she could, but nothing would happen until well after he got what was due to him. She had hit a raw nerve. His fingerprints of course later revealed he was 19 and wanted for other offences, with a lot of previous as well.

13

Interviewing Prisoners

Prior to the Police and Criminal Evidence Act (PACE), whenever a police officer interviewed a suspect, it had to be done contemporaneously. This meant that every single question was written down and so was every answer. Finally the suspect would have a chance to read it all over to ensure that they weren't being 'stitched up' and initialled every answer as being correct. If they wished they could, add, alter or delete anything. Finally, at the bottom of each page they would sign to say it was all correct. It was a long, painful and arduous task. To make matters worse, before PACE, little consideration was given to whether a prisoner was capable of doing this or not. Irrespective of their reading ability, we just slowly went through the procedure.

With the advent of PACE this was corrected and the custody sergeant would have to consider a number of things to ensure that the prisoner was being treated fairly and made aware of their rights, which included telling someone they had been arrested and getting legal advice. Before that, though, the sergeant would have to consider if the arresting officer had provided sufficient evidence for them to authorise the prisoner's further detention. The reason for the detention would be added to the custody sheet, and would include whether there was a need for further investigation, witness statements and an interview.

In order for all police officers to understand PACE, which involved huge changes to the method in which we policed and affected police powers, much for the better in some cases, we had to be trained. I along with my colleagues were sent on a whole afternoon of training, to be given an insight into a fair portion of the 120 sections that made up the Act.

During this particular afternoon I asked a simple question regarding our powers to stop and search and how this would differ from the current method and where we would actually record the stop, which clearly was different from the book we were using at the time. It was immediately obvious at this point that the training sergeant (I don't know if he had been an instructor at Hendon prior to this) actually didn't know the answer. Instead of just saying that this would all be clarified later he began to ramble on about silly questions and the need to just get on with it and for me to stop being a nuisance and asking mundane questions, despite his offer to answer any questions at the start.

Further training came when our contemporaneous interview records were to be replaced with a modern all singing and dancing tape-recording machine. Policing was sprinting its way in to the twentieth century in time to meet the twenty-first.

On my trip out to complete this training, we were given the run through of the system as well as being told the importance of showing the suspect that the tapes had never been used before. This would be followed by you breaking the seals, putting the two tapes into the machine and pressing the start button. In our case, the tape machine didn't work, so the instructor told us to imagine a long beep, at the end of which you would commence introductions followed by the interview. At the end of the interview one of the tapes would be sealed and placed in the property store and the other would act as the working copy. I managed to keep up and we were ready to be unleashed on the unsuspecting prisoners that we would be dealing with in the coming weeks.

One prisoner that I personally dealt with was another regular (if it wasn't him it was his brother, or if not him, both of them). As Chris was a young person he was accompanied by his mother. She was a colourful character. As per instructions I showed them both the new tapes and opened them in their presence and pressed the required button, which was followed by a high pitched noise, which I had explained to them both beforehand. This lasts for about ten seconds and during this time I very kindly (at least I thought so) told Chris that he still had his baseball cap on back to front and the machine was about to start. With this he quickly grabbed his cap and put it on correctly. At this point the bleep finished, with mum shouting, 'You fick bastard, it's a fu**ing tape recorder, not a fu**ing video recorder.' I then announced for the benefit of the tape that the interview was about to commence and the voice just heard was that of mum. I then introduced myself and asked Chris to supply his full name, also for the benefit of the tape, which he obligingly did.

On another occasion I had cause to arrest another regular. My mum always told me try to be regular, and this group certainly were. Again due to his age he was accompanied by mum who had a tracheotomy but it didn't impede her ability to act as the appropriate adult. After the now all too familiar introductions I began to ask a number of questions relating to the offence, in this case criminal damage to parking meters (sawing the tops off and removing the coins inside). The cost of the damage to the meter was always far greater than the theft. The young lad did very well answering all the questions, but when we got to the difficult questions he gave a very small laugh-come-hiccup before supplying his answer. Eventually I said, 'Do you always make that little laughing sound, just before you lie?' 'Hah,' (laugh, hiccup), 'no,' he replied. With this his mum interrupted and said, 'Yes you bleeding do, he's always done it.' Isn't that so much easier than writing – you see, not all change is bad, is it? The glass is half full, not half empty.

Some officers can be a little over-zealous about their duties. I was the custody sergeant one day when a PC returned from the interview room, explaining how frustrated he was with his prisoner because they were not giving a direct answer to a direct question.

In fact he was doing anything and everything possible to avoid helping – not surprising really, is it? Finally, at the end of the interview, with the tape still playing, the officer declared he'd heard enough nonsense, so the prisoner could go back to his cell, while he on the other hand was going to go home, have a nice cold lager, accompanied by a curry and with the last thought as he climbed into his nice warm bed being the simple fact that the prisoner wouldn't be getting any of that and at best would be facing a cold breakfast, whilst further enquiries would be made and another interview held later. The prisoner's solicitor confirmed this to me when she later came out of the interview room. This form of questioning is what was described to me at training school as being 'oppressive' and a court would undoubtedly decide that any information obtained in such a manner should be dismissed, which I carefully imparted to the officer for future reference.

14

Aid

In my first few years on the job I spent a lot of my time doing 'aid', as it is commonly known. Aid consists of dealing with demonstrations, football matches and ceremonial duties.

Aid invariably coincided with a trip to Central London and some hours later being returned with a familiar chant ringing in your ears ('Maggie, Maggie, Maggie, out, out, out!'). The hard core at the front supported just about every anti-government cause. I was seeing some of them more than my friends, I don't think they wanted to add any of us coppers to their Christmas card list though.

These trips would often be spent on an old coach known as a Green Goddess. Although these were used for normal marches, they were always used at this time to carry officers who formed the shield serials, as we stored all the shields in the back of the coach. They were damn uncomfortable, but officers always managed to set up a card table somehow with four officers playing from my station a game called 'Contract'. Other stations would have their own preferred game. Generally you started off with thirteen cards each, reducing to twelve, then eleven, until you got to two and if you wanted you could work your way back up to thirteen again. Each player had to nominate how many tricks they could win, but you couldn't have as many tricks as that particular hand. For example, if there were thirteen cards you could nominate any number of tricks between the four of you providing they didn't total the same as the amount of cards dealt out. This meant that at least one player would not make their nominated number of tricks. The person who nominated the highest number was able to call trumps. You got a point for each trick you won plus another ten points if you successfully managed to get the number of tricks you nominated at the start of the hand. The winner was the one with the most points at the end of the game.

I have never been much good at cards, but some of the guys took it very seriously, holding post-mortems after each hand and blaming someone for making ridiculous calls, but it broke up what could otherwise have been an even longer day.

Cards was also important to our morale when we went to the miners' strike demonstrations. I went twice and they were both very different occasions. The first was with a load of old sweats and the second was part of a shield serial. Before we could leave the Met for our deployment all the Met serials had to parade at Hendon. On the first occasion my chief superintendent was the senior officer in charge for the Met serials. He gave all the inspectors in charge of a serial a little talk before we departed for our respective postings. This included how he expected each and every officer to conduct themselves as he would and treat our host constabularies with politeness and good grace. When he arrived and was shown his own little quarters he demanded to know why an officer of his rank was being treated so appallingly. Oh dear. He did manage to get a mention in a police magazine at the time, which was the least he deserved.

On both the occasions I visited I went to Shirebrook colliery and like many other officers who went there I still have a memento on my key ring to this day. When a miner descended into the pit he would be handed a token and this would be collected when he left. Officers like me were getting their shoulder numbers engraved on one of these as a reminder of their involvement. There have been books and programmes made on the rights and wrongs of this dispute and I certainly do not wish to make any comment on that here.

I can say that in my experience the food was absolutely excellent.

We were working about a sixteen-hour shift including the travelling and we started the day with a huge breakfast at a local police station. When we got back to our lodgings we were fed by the armed forces with all manner of fantastic meals. My first stay had been at a Victorian maternity hospital, with cold running water. It certainly did have a feel of Victoriana about it. The second trip I was billeted in an RAF barracks, with about 150 officers to a room. We were also given a large box of snacks to sustain us during the day, which comprised of a sandwich, crisps, a chocolate bar and a bottle of water. This must have been in stark contrast to the families suffering throughout this time. The local kids use to come along to the police coaches and probably every officer on my coach handed their snacks over every day to the kids, minus the water. I presume and hope they took them back to their mums to share out amongst all the family.

It was during this time that I came to witness many of the other police forces marching around between their deployments. The Met on the other hand accepted that we were no good at marching, having left it behind at training school, so we just wandered or huddled towards our deployments. On one occasion we were lining a road expecting some trouble when a local superintendent appeared. I could tell he was a superintendent because he had a crown on his coat. Things must have been getting desperate at his force, because his mackintosh looked reminiscent of an old black and white movie and he was being followed in correct order by his staff officer. He looked like he was ready for business though as he had a swagger stick tucked beneath one arm. I had never seen this since leaving training school. As he began to move down our line he certainly looked ready to deal with any officer who was incorrectly dressed. Although he started off slowly and meaning-fully he began to pick up speed as the Met serials began to cheer louder and louder until he disappeared from view.

At this time the Met had small round stickers with 'I've met the Met' on them. These were handed out generally by officers visiting local schools but they were becoming the bane of the local constabularies' lives as they found them stuck just about every-where. Even the chief constable found he had one in his office after giving out a clear warning of the punishment if he caught anyone. Officers were going to no end of trouble and risk to ensure that nowhere was left without one, including a field of cows.

In the first half of my service you would go on a march or demonstration and you would find yourself on your coach with a large number of smokers. I have never smoked, although I have, like many of my other non-smoking colleagues, been a very active passive smoker. These old farts not only liked to smoke, they also had a hatred for any form of fresh air, and God help you if you wanted to open a window. Of course this has all changed now and thank goodness. If you want a fag you have to get off the coach; why should fifty of you all go home stinking of fags? Rant over.

Some years later as the sergeant in charge of a serial on aid, one of the PCs went to light his cigarette up on the coach. With this someone else used the well known analogy of 'he liked a beer, but didn't p**s on anyone afterwards', so why should he have to suffer the after-effects of smoking. Very quickly I was asked to make a decision, with a number of officers shouting out their opinion.

'OK, OK everyone, we are all grown people, we live in a democratic country we shall take a vote on it.' I counted the hands for, quickly followed by those against. 'There you have it everyone, democracy prevails, if you want to smoke get off the coach.' With this our smoker decided to complain, so I quickly interrupted stating that I had fifteen years' service and in all of that time no fu**er who smoked bothered about me. Therefore as democracy had failed I would use the other simple solution. I was in charge of the serial and until someone senior in rank overruled me, for the next fifteen years I would even things out. So I finished quite simply with, 'Confucius he say tough shit, off the coach.'

I have enjoyed the occasions on which I have had the good fortune to police Remembrance Sunday. It's a privilege to be reminded of sacrifices during the two world wars and those of recent times as you watch ex-servicemen and women march past. I also policed the wedding of Prince Charles to Lady Diana, Trooping the Colour and many other well-known events. Who said policing wasn't fun?

15

Paperwork, Paperwork

At varying stages over the years a number of governments have said they would reduce bureaucracy for the police and no doubt this will continue for many years to come. There is absolutely no doubt that there is heaps more paperwork now than when I joined.

We had a lovely system: if you had a crime arrest you had to complete a form 611. This was a four-sided cardboard document that would also hold the other papers relating to the case. This form required the personal details of the prisoner, brief details of the offence, the make-up of their family, details of their job and income and added to this would be details of convictions for the last three years. There was sufficient information for the matter to be dealt with at the first court hearing if necessary.

The only real pain at this time was the need to complete form 78, detailing all the personal details of the suspect: name, address, age, height, build etc., what the suspect had been wearing, any tattoos, the method used to commit the offence. This information would be sent to a department at Scotland Yard. There was also the need to ensure that there was a duplicate copy. The form also had to be completed on a typewriter. This created two problems: finding some carbon paper regardless of quality, and locating a working typewriter, preferably with a typewriter ribbon that still enabled you to complete the form. I would be very surprised if any officer ever witnessed the ribbons being replaced with a new one after the original purchase of the machine. I have witnessed many things in the job, but I have certainly not witnessed a typewriter ribbon replacement, why that could cripple a budget! Finance departments would be closing doors and taking telephones off the hook at the mere mention of the word.

One day one of my forms was returned to me with a nice memo that had been signed 'pp commander of the respective department', which stated that I had failed to meet the required standard and I would have to resubmit the form. I am quite fortunate because I can type, so this was not too arduous a job, but it is tiring when in the middle of the night you cannot get into half the offices, not that I can blame them because some lazy sod would only run out to a call and leave the remains of a half-eaten curry or Chinese there.

Nothing else for it, so I found the worst piece of carbon paper in the station (it was a close run thing, and there were a lot of candidates). I examined both the typewriters (again it was a close run thing) and chose the worst available. I completed the necessary form and attached it with my original. I then typed out a short memo, stating that I had completed another form as requested, on this occasion using the other available machine and a different piece of carbon paper, stating that unfortunately we did not have any new carbon available. I also apologised for the poor quality but I was in a quandary as I and others had tried to get decent equipment, all to no avail. If however the commander could intervene I and many of my colleagues would be forever grateful and no doubt the quality of work from our station would increase tenfold. I didn't hear anything and the equipment remained with us, a bit like a family heirloom that you would like to throw out, but can't quite bring yourself to do so.

When our typing ladies were moved from our station I requested on a formal report that the teams be allowed to have access to these fine electrical machines and cited the above example as one of the many benefits. The file was returned from our finance department with the comment 'These are expensive machines and officers are not suitably trained and cannot be trusted'. How very very dare you.

At about the same time I broke my wrist and was off work for a few weeks. Upon my return I found the station had suffered an outbreak of a computer virus. I'm sure some geek will be able to identify the correct term, but with absolutely no training on electric typewriters we had suddenly suffered an outbreak of computers – all over the station they were. All we needed was a log in and away we could go. What the hell was a log in? It was hilarious really, but at last we had something that would allow you to do reports in a professional manner. Not our 78s though, that system had to remain for the time being. We'll get there in small bites I was told.

I on the other hand took a bit longer. Having been provided with the power of a password I went to log myself on. After a few attempts I was told I had been locked out, but I hadn't even got in, was someone winding me up? It was dam well working. This was like being back home with your parents, warned of the consequences if you weren't in by a certain time. In this case it had happened, and I'd been locked out. Frustrated and angry I went to the person who was in charge of these things who ran a number of questions past me until they established I had made a very common error – I had had the capital lock key on instead of off. Oh really, did I look that interested? I only wanted an electric typewriter, I could operate those.

A few weeks later and I was at our main station and completed a letter that I needed to send off urgently. I pressed 'print', walked to the printer, no letter. I returned to carry this out again with the same result when someone asked if it had paper. A quick check revealed we were full of A4 and we should have been ready to rock and roll. What on earth was wrong with the bloody thing? Of course there was nothing wrong with it as you no doubt know – it was me. I'd had enough so I hit the print key as fast as I could for about ten seconds. It still hadn't printed so I resorted to an old favourite, and went to the canteen for a cup of tea and sod the expense: I'd have some toast as well.

I had barely taken the first sip of tea when Peggy appeared and scanned the canteen until her eyes fell on me. Not in that longing and loving way you sometimes witness, oh no, this was very much different to that. No cooing words either, just simply, 'You,' (that meant me) 'you're responsible for this.' And with this she waved all sixty copies of my letter at me. 'Come on. With me right this instant.' She was being very forceful, I didn't even dare to mention I would like to finish my tea and toast, so I was escorted to the typing pool where I was educated in how you selected the printer you wanted your documents to print to. There were choices? How did you choose? I thought it automatically printed to the nearest machine. Oh dear. The finance manager had been correct all along; I hadn't been trained and I couldn't be trusted. I take it all back.

Appraisals are the bane of any supervisor's life. In many cases you set objectives that you know have little or no chance of ever being achieved, which is exactly what they should be in the first place, according to the policy. After completing my probation I fell into the annual appraisal system, which was completed on the anniversary of the date you joined the Force. This involved a chat with your team inspector prior to facing a senior officer. Clearly it was important to identify weaknesses and how you could work on them to improve.

At about the stage of four years' service I had spent six months in a small police office, with just a sergeant in charge, but much of the time you were left to your own devices. For this reason I decided to keep a record of everything that I did in case I was challenged by one of the bosses. Amongst other things I had managed over sixty arrests, many for simple crimes such as shoplifting, people wanted on warrant and minor assaults.

A couple of weeks after returning to the team I had to take one of the probationers, Jim, with me. During our patrol I spotted a young lad and as I drove past slowly I caught a flash from his finger, which immediately raised my suspicions. Jim and I stopped the young lad and along with the nice flashy ladies' diamond ring on his finger he had several others in his pocket. This earned him a free ride in my car back to the station. It later transpired that he had committed a burglary a few miles away. During the booking-in procedure the superintendent visited the charge room and commented on what a good job we had done.

Two weeks later I found myself in front of the superintendent as he went through my appraisal, with him commenting on the number of arrests. He pointed out that I shouldn't get ahead of myself because it wasn't difficult to arrest shoplifters. I replied it was if you didn't accept the calls, which some officers were slower in doing than others.

Moving on he stated that the number of arrests was not outstanding, indeed any officer could do similar. I began to get a bit defensive at this stage because I wasn't looking for a posting anywhere, but I thought I could be told that I was doing all right and to keep it up. My mental arithmetic was probably my strong suit at school, so I very quickly told him that last year approximately 6,000 people had visited our cells and if his comment was correct, taking into account the number of officers at the station, he was another 6,000 arrests short. I think at this stage it became a case of he was a senior officer and there was only going to be one winner. One thing to remember with bosses though, they may not always be right, but they are always the boss.

'OK then,' he said, 'when was the last occasion that you generated an arrest of your own, rather than from taking a call?' I thought for a brief moment and suddenly remembered my little burglar, so I recounted this, explaining that several thousand pounds worth of jewellery had been recovered and the good superintendent had commented on it. I think in chess terms this would be called checkmate. Oh no, defeat could not be that easy. 'I don't recall that,' he said.

I'd had enough now, there were many areas that I was lacking in, many of which I was acutely aware of, and if he had wished to delve a little deeper I am sure he would quickly have found one or two, so I said, 'You are telling me sir that you as a senior officer cannot recall an incident that only happened two weeks ago.'

The conversation was brought to an abrupt end as the superintendent threw me out of the office, shouting about how on earth I had the audacity to question a senior officer like that. I had perhaps not been very diplomatic, perhaps that could have been a development area for me.

Oh dear.

I managed to get thrown out the next year as well. I wouldn't mind but I was genuinely not trying to annoy him. In fact I thought he was a decent boss, he generally asked pertinent questions and seemed interested.

As per the script I met with my inspector (duty officer) to discuss my annual performance. He had been with us for six months and was a fair governor. I think he was responsible for sowing the seeds of doubt with me regarding appraisals. As he sat back in his office with his tie off and feet on his desk, he explained the way he had been taught to conduct such interviews when he completed his inspectors' course some several months earlier.

'What you are instructed to do Smithy is to take control of the meeting. You should sit higher than the person you are interviewing, therefore making them feel inferior, giving you a position of control to dominate proceedings; what a load of old crap. When I did my practical they sent this tasty bird in, who was on her sergeants' course. She can come on this team any time she likes I can tell you, what a looker. Anyway, they play their silly games and she is given her brief, and I've been told she has been failing in some areas and I have to decide what the way forward is. As I challenge her, she raises her skirt a little, which I must say made me get my legs off the table and sit up properly. She then fluttered her eyes at me and said we hadn't been out on a team drink and perhaps we should. So I told her, what a good idea.'

Apparently they didn't seem to like that approach.

My final appraisal at the station and again I was seated before the superintendent who was about four inches shorter than me. As I sat down I was a little higher in my seat than him seated in his posh senior officer's seat, so he adjusted it accordingly, placing him higher than me. The conversation with my inspector immediately came back to my mind. I then adjusted my seat so that I was again fractionally above the superintendent, which he quickly remedied. Unfortunately I couldn't raise my chair any further so I lowered it instead right to the bottom setting, which now left a huge difference between our seating positions. Clearly they hadn't explained such behaviour on any courses at this time, but to be fair he did get on with the job.

He informed me that he was forever getting letters of complaint from councillors about the failure by his station to deal with the ever-increasing abuse of the yellow lines around the town. Some years later the councillors dealt with the problem once and for all, they pedestrianised it. Why didn't the super think of that?

'Just what do you do when you are on patrol along the high street and notice a large number of cars illegally parked? And don't tell me you just walk past.'

'Well sir, when I do have the time I walk along a line of cars slowly to make sure that my presence is noticed first and foremost. I believe this prevents others from also thinking of parking and making matters worse. I look into one or two of the shops and I make a bit of fuss about getting my pen and tickets out. If by now there is not a hive of activity with all the car owners scurrying to their cars, shouting apologies, I may issue a ticket.' In truth I didn't always carry them because they were rather bulky. I couldn't look untidy, I had learnt that from Bomber. Apparently this was exactly the kind of attitude that the superintendent had to defeat and he would make a start with me. So I would have to pull my socks up, indeed he would be checking on all the officers, the duty officers would be tasked. He clearly meant it.

I assured the boss that I would do my best but I did indeed have a solution to his problem. A few weeks before my appraisal one of our police magazines reported that the average traffic warden was issuing on average two parking tickets per day. I personally didn't think this was particularly good, unless I was the motorist parked on the yellow line of course, because I happened to be a local lad.

Of course the rules of the day required the traffic warden to note the position of the valves on the tyres, note the time, and check on the vehicle later before issuing a ticket. Alternatively they could observe the vehicle for sufficient time to ensure that it was not loading or unloading and at that time issue a ticket as per their training.

These incidents would result in the traffic wardens writing their tickets up before or after their allotted mealbreaks. I personally would love to see the return of the traffic warden – they at least could use the power of discretion, although they still patrol the red routes for the moment. The modern replacement on the other hand has a simple mission to complete as many as possible. There is no discretion, not that I am bitter and twisted of course, and have never been the recipient of any tickets for illegal parking, oh no.

Oh dear.

The superintendent, believing I had an answer to one of his problems, eyed me suspiciously and clearly thinking better of it asked me anyway, just how I could solve the problem. 'Quite easy sir, I would walk over to the canteen, direct all the traffic wardens out onto their beats and to produce more than two tickets per day, as per the average, which was mentioned recently in the *Job*.' End of appraisal, I had gone too far, I was being flippant and my duty officer would be updated. Indeed he was updated and he roared, particularly when I told him he had been correct about the psychobabble with the chair.

I think the appraisal system has changed just about every year in the last ten. The current system, if followed correctly, should see the person being appraised presenting their collection of evidence to their boss, or line manager. This allows a two-way flow, thereby ensuring that a fair report is completed, reflecting the work of the member of staff throughout the year.

Additionally, if you are responsible for any officers or staff you should also maintain details of all the evidence relating to each person. I think this is fair; it certainly saves a busy sergeant having the onus put on them and likewise allows individuals to have the opportunity of a fair report.

A few months after I left a team they received a newly-qualified sergeant, who by the sounds of things was keen to ensure that these administrative tasks were completed as per instructions. He announced that each and every person that he had to report on would be expected to provide a portfolio of their work. Any failure to do this would see the requisite comments and marks being placed on their official file. 'What a load of old bo**ocks,' Kevin said. 'I've got over twenty-five years' service, I'm still doing earlics, lates and nights, I answer any calls that are given to me and besides I've just come back from Traffic Division, so I doubt I shall be specialising any more.'

At this point the sergeant made himself quite clear on the matter and the approach that he would be taking. (He may have been looking for a job at the training school.) Sure enough the day arrived when Kevin had to have his appraisal. Both officers sat down and Kevin, as requested, produced his evidence for the year, which totalled about a four-inch thick binder, complete with all the work he had undertaken whilst he was at Traffic, including reports to local authorities regarding road layouts, minutes of the meetings he had attended, a copy of large amounts of calls that he had dealt with, along with a list of intelligence reference numbers as well as custody numbers.

The sergeant enquired what this was all about. Was Kevin having a laugh? 'No Sarge, I thought about what you said and thought I should value myself and the results of my labours. All of last night duty I volunteered to be station officer and while I was out of the way I put this all together.'

'But I haven't got time to go through all of this,' complained the sergeant.

'Oh yes you will Sarge, and the rest of the team are also

following my example, exactly as you directed. Please make sure that my report is properly reflected won't you, and I shall be more than happy to discuss this in more detail with you when you are ready to.'

Sometimes you should be careful for what you wish for.

I had the task of completing an appraisal for a PC on my team, Len, who had just completed his thirty years' service. Although he was eligible to retire he loved the job and wanted to continue driving the area car. Len told me that I could write what I wanted, so I did. The report finished: 'Len now feels that after thirty years' service he has the confidence to look towards promotion and intends to take the sergeants' exam next year.' Nobody ever asked if I was being serious, I think Len and I were the only ones who read it.

When I worked on another team one of the PCs, Phil, was again nearing retirement but we went through the usual ritual, which included a comment I made about his diligence to apprehend a wanted villain. Originally Phil had contacted the wanted bloke on his mobile phone and he had agreed to attend the station not once but twice, before our suspect told Phil that he could f**k off. Clearly Phil didn't know where he lived otherwise he would have been around by now, besides he didn't live on the manor so he was stuffed. With this the phone was slammed down.

Phil was outraged. He had attempted to treat this man with fairness and respect, offering to get him to court with the warrant as soon as possible, rather than spend a weekend in the pokey (another name for cell), and what had he got for it? Abuse. As this was now personal Phil trawled through all the databases, finally locating his man a couple of Divisions away. The next available morning nice and early Phil knocked at the suspect's door, which was eventually answered, and before he could even be cautioned, those immortal words were heard, 'Oh f**ck.' He wasn't wrong.

Eighteen months after capturing this for posterity on the required form I went to Phil's retirement drinks. The superintendent was doing the leaving speech and cited from the latest appraisal a story of the determination that Phil had only recently displayed to apprehend a wanted villain. This all began to sound very familiar, but I had written that particular report well over eighteen months ago and another appraisal would have been done since then. As I thought this my eye was caught by another sergeant standing across the bar who was smiling at me and displaying two fingers in a cutting motion and then pretending to lick a piece of paper as she mouthed, 'Cut and paste.' The cheeky cow had just changed the date, why hadn't I thought of that? Bloody clever these women.

As well as completing police officer appraisals I have completed appraisals for police staff, affectionately known as 'civvies', but that is not conducive to the modern world, hence the title 'police staff'. At this time they were all completed at the same time of the year, so this meant a lot of time and effort. If the civilian member of staff could evidence that their work was above the required standard they would get a small financial reward. This has changed now and could be divisive amongst the teams.

I met this retired police officer who was now doing a civilian role. I reminded him of the rules and that I would be fair if he provided the evidence. He looked at me as many old sweats have done with their supervisors over the years and said, 'Guv'nor there's no point, I won't get what I deserve, I don't need the extra couple of pounds and besides there is nothing anyone can tell me about this job, in fact I can walk on water according to some.'

'Well Harry I like the sound of that. I know of only one previous recording of walking on water and I would love to witness it. I had to walk through a bloody great puddle to get in to your office today, so if you can walk on that I'll give you the top grading and I'll write it out before I leave.'

With this he smiled and said, 'Well you've got a sense of humour, so I'll make the tea.' Good man, he still hadn't forgotten how the job worked thank goodness.

16

Domestic Incidents

This is an area which has changed considerably over the years. Way back when, you would go along and arbitrate between the couple, then leave. If there was a need you would make an arrest for assault, but this was made difficult with predominantly women declining to provide a statement and attend court, probably with good cause, namely fear of getting more of the same when the old man returned home the next day.

As the police reviewed their working practices we began to report every incident as a crime and over the course of time I believe that we have become far more professional, indeed generally an arrest is made. That said, the 'one size fits all' approach doesn't always work. Like many of my colleagues I have dealt with some complete arseholes and I enjoyed every moment when I was able to arrest some violent bully who terrified their family.

One of the first calls that I attended was about two in the morning at a high-rise block of flats. The call to the police had been made by a neighbour who had to be up for work in a few hours and wanted the rowing couple to be told to quieten down. As I was being driven there, my colleague, Mick, explained that there were a couple of things that would be the curse of my or any other officer's working life: juveniles at all times, and their parents at domestic incidents.

Pretty quickly we found ourselves at the correct flat. The argument was still ongoing but there were no sounds of obvious violence. This was all confirmed when our knock at the door was answered and we were ushered inside. Mick asked the warring pair what the problem was and it transpired that they were not married and the council flat was in the lady's name and she sub-let one of the rooms. In return for board and lodging the services for the week also included sandwiches for the lodger, which he took to work.

'So what is the problem then?' Mick asked the man.

'Well I keep telling her, I like cheese sandwiches, but occasionally I would like something different, I don't want cheese every bloody day, otherwise there's never anything to look forward to. I work hard on the building site and when I have me break it's nice to sit down with me cup of tea and guess what will be in me lunch box? Today when I opened me box I had *jam* sandwiches, how is that going to sustain a bloke of my size doing a hard day's work? When I said something different from cheese, I didn't mean bloody jam, kids eat jam sandwiches, not grown working men.'

With this the woman started interrupting and began to threaten the man with eviction, which led to the two of them back at each other's throats again despite the presence of Mick and me. With a shout from Mick the two were brought under control as the whole sorry saga was repeated again. I found this all surreal, it was like a sketch out of *The Two Ronnies*, as the middle-aged pair both blamed each other.

Finally Mick took control with a loud shout. As a married man himself he had some understanding I presumed of both parties' point of view. 'Right I've heard enough, the whole bloody block of flats will be up here in a minute. I don't want any talk of throwing people out, otherwise the council can find out you're sub-letting and you won't be far behind being thrown out of the flat yourself. Secondly, what is the problem in occasionally giving your lodger a corned beef or ham sandwich, instead of cheese? If there is any extra cost then surely you can discuss that between you. Is that understood?'

Finally they both nodded and as we made our way back to the nick it was time for me to complete my tea-making duty. When I got back I explained that the single life didn't appear to be too bad. I certainly was not ready for arguments over jam or cheese sandwiches at two o'clock in the morning. With this JD said, 'I tell you what we need. We need some domestic harmony around here ourselves.' He looked at me. 'I tell you what boy, as the chair and secretary of the tea club and due to the fact we have some extra milk, I am going to give you the authority to make us all a nice milky coffee.'

Off I toddled in an attempt to maintain the harmony of the team. It was a rare occasion a generous moment for JD, who for once had lost brief sight of the cost to his beloved tea club.

Generally in my experience, on a call to a domestic incident with violence involved you will find the victim is female. On one occasion however I attended a flat and found a well-spoken couple, both clearly not drunk and no signs of a disturbance in the well-kept home. The man informed me that his wife had promised she was going to cut off his genitals and he was scared to go to sleep because he knew she would do it. With this the well-dressed lady explained that she had been out with a lady friend and they had returned to her home to find her husband walking around in his boxer shorts. He then began to make crude remarks and began to thrust his groin out – in some sort of ancient ritual to drive women crazy I presume. It clearly didn't work. His wife explained that she asked him to behave in a more gentlemanly manner and to stop embarrassing himself, and her that he should desist, which after some time he eventually did.

Once the friend had left the flat the lady told her husband that she had never been so embarrassed in her life and that she would remove the offending articles as earlier stated. I told them both to calm down and that in the heat of the moment we all say things that we regret, but now we needed to take a deep breath and think clearly.

With this the man said, 'Oh she means it, she always carries out her threats, look.' He undid his shirt and showed me where she had put a heated iron on his chest some years ago. Clearly emblazoned on his chest was the complete mark of an iron. This took the saying 'don't get mad get even' too far. She didn't want counselling as she didn't perceive it to be a problem, so I advised him to seek advice from a solicitor as these matters only ever escalate, they rarely self-correct.

I worked at one station where a gay couple were always having domestic incidents. They were a strange couple to say the least. They comprised of Wayne and his partner Rita, who I only ever saw in a frock, something similar to the get up Les Dawson used to wear in his Cissie and Ada sketches. In fact Rita could have played Les Dawson's twin sister and become the addition to Cissie and Ada. Rita always seemed to need a shave and had a permanent five o'clock shadow and no teeth, although they may have been at the side of the bed, I never did find out, thankfully. You had to address him as 'Rita' otherwise he would get upset. It certainly takes all sorts. This day we got a call early in the morning before they had had a chance to start drinking or even find something to disagree on, at least that is what you would have thought.

The pair lived near the top of a tower block and usually the victim would be Rita, plus her five o'clock shadow, and we would cart Wayne away, until Rita would refuse to provide a statement because he loved him. This day however Wayne had already made a speedy exit before our arrival and Rita stood in his doorway with a tear in his eye and arms crossed. He definitely looked like something out of a Les Dawson sketch. To make matters worse he hadn't put his teeth in at this stage. 'What's the matter this time Rita?'

In his northern accent, exaggerated by his lack of teeth, and looking sorry for himself, Rita explained. 'Well officer, normally it's Wayne what assaults me as you know. But today he got up and started on me immediately for no good reason, God knows I try me best for 'im, but I'd 'ad enough. So I 'it 'im with the frying pan and told 'im not to darken me door again and that's when he ran out of the flat.' With this Rita put both skinny arms out in front of him and told me that he would understand. 'It's ok officer I know you've got to arrest me, you've got your job to do.'

'Rita, God only knows what you have had to put up with love. On this occasion I am not going to arrest you, I think you deserve some peace and quiet. While he is out of the flat, hopefully Wayne is reflecting on the way he has treated you. Who knows, perhaps he will mend his ways. You take care and let's try not to get called back. You know the number if he causes any problems.'

'Oh thank you officer, it's very good of you, I was sure I was going to get banged up after I whacked him one.' With this we left satisfied that there were no other immediate problems requiring our attention.

The following week of course we had a return call and Wayne was duly arrested and brought to the custody suite where I was the custody officer. Len had provided me with all the details of the domestic incident, whereupon Wayne called Len 'a bald-headed bastard'. Len immediately retorted in Churchillian style: 'I may be bald, but in the morning you will still be gay.' Wayne looked lost for words, they were of course both correct, but it made the rest of us in the charge room laugh.

For many years my day-to-day policing took place on estates in the south-east boroughs of London. I had been doing an office job for just over a year and felt that I needed to go back to daily policing, but also felt that I needed to go somewhere else and experience a different environment. I quickly found myself working in Central London as a duty officer.

The reality of the difference between the two areas was brought home to me one night duty when a call came out to a family dispute. A male had been assaulted and the location was a very very expensive area. An ambulance had been called and police units were also assigned. There were clear guidelines on how these incidents should now be treated, so I thought I would take a slow wander to the incident and get to know the ground at the same time.

When I arrived the officers quickly explained that there were three parties involved: the victim who needed to go to hospital and the two suspects, a middle-aged lady and her nephew. There seemed to be a lot of messing around so I asked why we needed to remain at the scene and I found I was being told about the needs of the dog, how it was terribly inconvenient, until I had heard enough and directed that the suspects should be taken to the station where it could all be arranged there, we needed to get on with things.

I followed the police cars back to the station and as I got out of my car in the yard the female asked me where she had to go now. She was very well-spoken and no doubt a very pleasant lady normally, so I pointed to a door which led to the custody suite and told her.

'You will be going there and you will have all your rights explained to you. Additionally you can call someone to see to your dog.'

With this she looked absolutely flabbergasted, but quickly recovered and said, 'But I can't possibly go in there, I am dressed from head to toe in Armani.'

I was clearly no longer working the estates of south-east London, which I was beginning to miss.

17

Car Chases and Accidents

When I first heard a police chase on the police radio I knew that I wanted to be involved in that, rather than slowly walking around my designated beat. It is adrenalin-pumping stuff as I found out the first time I was involved in one. I was the operator on the area car when the driver spotted a motorcycle two-up and indicated for it to pull over. Of course it accelerated away very quickly. I began to call up on the R/T set to MP that we had a motorcycle two-up failing to stop. I kept telling myself to keep calm, communicate in a steady voice. I don't know if I managed this or not, nobody took the mickey after so I suppose I did all right. But the bike was getting away, and Geoff was now picking up speed as we drove through the London streets in the early hours at a very high rate of knots.

As we got onto a main road the bike couldn't pull away from us, but it had a good head start as we began to go up a hill and through a red traffic light. Why risk your life for something like this? It's ridiculous even if you are not worried about the safety of anyone else, but it happens all too often.

Two thirds of the way up the hill we had only been going for about three minutes when the bike turned off into a side road and as we followed around the corner the bike was lying in the road. Obviously with the layout of the road both suspects had gone into some woods. The one distinctive difference between the driver and pillion was the colour of the helmets.

The area was cordoned and a short while later with the dog van in attendance we managed to find the driver. My heart was still going as fast as our car, my first, albeit short, chase was over. The bike had been stolen and we had one in custody – yes, this was more like it.

Two days after I passed my own driving course I saw a car four-up near an estate. You didn't need to be a top detective to know that we needed to have a chat. They had other ideas so they sped off. I was alone, so you provide an update on the radio when it is safe to do so. This time I found myself speeding down a different hill.

There are two big differences between the police and the villain when it comes to car chases. Firstly, the police officer has been provided with some training; the old area car driver would have spent in total nine weeks completing the various courses before being trusted, if they reached the required standard, which they didn't all manage to. Secondly, and most importantly, you have the well-being of the public in mind. Officers generally won't take unnecessary risks despite the fact they want to catch the bad guys.

As we got to the bottom of the hill the bandit car, as it is often called, just went straight onto the dual carriageway, thankfully without hitting another car. I followed as I had been taught, continuing to provide updates as I could. After a few hundred yards the dual carriageway we were now on reduced to a single lane, which would not have been a problem if my sergeant hadn't pulled from one of the local problem estates in front of me. Fortunately I didn't rear end him, much to the disappointment of the locals at the nearby estate.

With this our area car came into action and at this time you fall back and allow them to do their job, they are far better equipped. I stayed with the chase, which was now out of my sight, and followed the radio transmission. I would imagine at this stage the driver of the bandit car knew he wasn't going to get away, so he also headed to a wooded area and the occupants did a starburst followed by the crew of the area car.

Now at this point the crew of the bandit car really did have some bad luck. As they made their way into the woods, unbeknown to them and us, the local CID were conducting an observation on an entirely different matter and collected all the occupants of the stolen car without even breaking into a sweat.

Similar to my first foot chase, I did not manage to get one of the arrests, but the good thing was it was Team Met 1, Bad guys 0.

Some years later as a sergeant I jumped into the back of the area car, which was being driven by a driver who had only just been reinstated after a lengthy suspension. As we slowly patrolled around a number of estates our attention was drawn to another car creeping around and very quickly it was game on.

After the bandit car tried to lose us around the small tight backroads he went onto a main road and I had no doubt that it was now game over as he was in a small car far less powerful than ours. It didn't end as I imagined or hoped though.

Approaching a set of lights at a very busy main arterial road the bandit car lost control and went to the offside of the road, colliding with a very sturdy metal bollard, which then sent him back across to the other side of the road at which point he went through a red traffic light. I winced in anticipation of an almighty crash, but it didn't happen as I had thought. Again, fortunately, there wasn't a car coming the other way, instead the bandit car swerved back to the near side of the road, now completely out of control. The bandit car hit the kerb and the front of the car rose as it hit a very large tree. At this point I can still see it in my mind's eye as the car began to take off into the air. It was like something out of a Bond movie. The car began to do a 180-degree turn as it now began to descend back to earth, with an almighty crash on its roof and skidded about a hundred yards before coming to a stop in the middle of the road. Fortunately nothing had been coming the other way, the results would have been too horrendous to contemplate.

Dick, our driver, stopped the car at the junction and I directed James, the operator, to cordon the road off as I ran to the car. I wasn't expecting to see a very nice sight. As I looked into the very crushed car the driver looked towards me, having been saved by not wearing a seat belt, and yelled, 'Get me out of this f**ing car you c**t!' As he said this I could see a very large piece of skin flapping about from his scalp. He looked a bit like one of the puppets on a Saturday morning programme some years ago, *Sage and Onion*.

After telling the driver to shut up and apply pressure to his flap, we cordoned the road off in case the driver later died of his injuries. This is known as a 'vicinity only' police accident and the traffic sergeant would be attending to investigate, amongst other things, if there was any blame on the part of the police driver. As if the bandit driver had not been fortunate enough, so far the car hadn't caught light because quite simply we couldn't have got him out. That was a job for the LFB who were very quickly on scene. The little toad was still aggressive when he got out and was taken to the local hospital. When he was eventually released from hospital some days later, what a scar – it looked as if he had been attacked by a shark – and to add insult to injury he had several charges to go with it.

18

General Duties but not Generally Trouble

You cannot be a police officer for too long before you hear of something funny, a ridiculous incident involving some local family, or a colleague doing something daft regardless of how well intentioned.

The number of characters in the job is probably no greater than any other, but they certainly help to make an ordinary day that much brighter. At one station I worked at there was a lot of building work being done and as there were not a lot of officers working out of the station the decision was made to put all the male and female lockers together. This obviously came with a number of concerns, so it was stressed that we all needed to be adult about it and a sensible approach was taken.

A female sergeant, whilst changing, noticed that one of the lads had a picture on the inside of his locker with a very attractive actress clad in a bikini. She couldn't have been having a good day, despite only just starting her shift, and removed the 'offending' item and tore it up. Later on she challenged the officer, Cliff, regarding his approach to depicting females in such a poor light.

This had not gone down very well at all and was the main discussion point over grub. Cliff stated it was out of order and something had to be done about it and it just so happened he knew what. Cliff approached the sergeant and clarified that his information was correct and that similar action would be taken against any other officer doing anything similar. 'I'm glad I clarified that sergeant and you should lead by example.' With this he grabbed her calendar from her desk which depicted a number of fit looking firemen semi-clad and holding their dripping hoses. With a swift yank the calendar was torn in half and dropped into the nearby waste-paper basket. 'There you go Sarge, I fully support you.' There was a great roar of laughter when he updated his mates. The sergeant was left gobsmacked and completely snookered. She had been caught out at her own game.

Shortly after this episode our female inspector had a traumatic incident. She had gained a couple of pounds over the years (I resemble this remark) as she was nearing her pension. As she joined her team for the start of the shift she explained that she was in her bra and knickers in the locker room when a builder's head appeared through a ceiling tile. 'I had to dive for cover,' she said.

Cliff very quickly responded, 'Has anyone got counselling for the builder?' Our inspector had a good sense of humour, so she just told him he was a cheeky sod and to hurry up and make her tea.

'No problem Ma'am, I'll just go and check on the builder first.'

A few months later the team was assisting in an annual duty providing some supervision on a day out for some local disabled youngsters. As we all waited for the off our inspector arrived dressed in a leopard-print suit. She was unaware that we were already waiting at the venue. While she stood on the busy road having a cigarette the quiet of the morning was broken by Fred shouting, 'I've told you before about standing on street corners, I won't tell you again. The next time you're coming into the nick,' indicating that she was a lady of the night, shall we say.

'You cheeky sod Fred, I thought better of you.'

'All right then, how much? It is a day for charity after all.'

Some months later and Fred came to me to discuss a problem on his beat. A bedsit in the local student accommodation appeared to be dealing drugs. We both went to see the caretaker and confirmed that this was the case. After further enquiries Fred got permission from our inspector to apply for a drug search warrant, which he obtained from the local court.

From the intelligence we gathered we confirmed that the students were both French, which wasn't too much of a problem as Simon on our team was fluent. He would be with us on the day, so if necessary we could overcome any minor language barrier until we got an official interpreter back at the nick. We identified a suitable late shift and as we had the key for the premises we didn't need any heavy-handed tactics, just a quick entry. As it was Fred's job he went first, but as he opened the door he just stood there announcing it was the police – he had become the local sheriff. Possibly the police uniform may have been a clue anyway, but we weren't getting control of the room, which was a problem as our two students were sitting at a kitchen table sharing out the drugs, which they kindly didn't scatter across the room. Fortunately we managed to move Fred into the room and arrested our pair of French drug dealers. Simon explained in perfectly accented French what was to happen, established they both spoke English, and a little while later they were escorted, handcuffed, out of the building.

We just had to search their car and then we would be making our way back to the nick. As Simon went off to do this the pair started to talk to each other in French. Well Fred had witnessed how good a job Simon had made of his interpreting skills earlier and just to show these French that the English could master another language Fred jumped straight in. I think 'shut up' would have done the trick, but this was a day for professionalism. Fred's version went something like this in a very heavy English accent: 'Non parle Francais, parle English por favour. Ya.' Fred was looking very pleased with himself. Well I knew we were in the EEC now, but what the hell was that all about? Still our two students shut up in disbelief as Cliff and I just doubled up with laughter.

'What's the matter with you two pair of wankers?' asked Fred.

'It's you Fred,' cried Cliff, 'I didn't realise you knew so many languages and all at once'. With this I just broke out with tears of laughter, quickly followed by Cliff.

'You pair of stupid c**ts.' Cliff and I were now hysterical as Fred escorted his prisoners away, looking a little bit hurt after an otherwise successful operation.

The following year and I had transferred to a day job. After twenty years of shift work I was having a break from front-line policing. No sooner had I got the job, when I was told it would probably only be for a few months as a review had just been announced, which would probably see a big overhaul.

Oh dear.

I was working with a small team of nice guys. One of them, Alan, had a lunchtime ritual. Five minutes before lunch and the kettle would be switched on. His sandwich box would be removed from the fridge, followed by him making several slow trips patrolling up and down the office, no doubt making sure no one was coming to take his grub and Cuppa Soup. Just before the signal that the kettle had boiled Alan would reveal his sandwiches, empty the Cuppa Soup into his mug, add boiling water, stir methodically, tuck his napkin into the top of his shirt, remove his glasses and enjoy. The simple pleasures in life.

This fine day all was going to plan until he opened his lunchbox to find he had no Cuppa Soup. 'OK lads you've had a laugh, now put it back please.' None of us knew what he was talking about at this stage and although he didn't believe us at first it came to dawn on him that the Cuppa Soup had actually been left out.

'Just go without it today Alan,' suggested one of the other guys. Eventually this is what he had to do, but he was like a child who just discovered he was no longer going to be breast fed. It was a sad day.

After a very sad lunchtime it was discovered that Alan's wife was away and she always made his lunches. On this occasion he had made it himself and only had himself to blame for his missing Cuppa Soup. The afternoon was a grumpy one. I'd had enough, action was required, and we couldn't go through another afternoon like that. I armed myself with a pen and paper and wrote a letter for home to the 55-year-old's wife.

Dear Anna, it is with some sadness that I have been forced to write to you to today, regarding some disturbing behaviour displayed by Alan this lunchtime. I understand that you are currently away and will not read this until the weekend. It has also come to my notice that you normally make Alan's lunchbox up, so he was forced to attempt this arduous duty whilst home alone. Today he forgot to bring his Cuppa Soup with him and I shall leave it for Alan to explain his behaviour, but it was clearly upsetting for him and we have been forced to live with him this afternoon, which has been very difficult indeed. I would hate to see him go through this again, or the rest of the team live through a similar incident. If you wouldn't mind sending me an emergency ration I shall ensure that it is kept safe should the need arise. I shall also monitor the best before dates. Hope you had a good break, I am sure you needed it. Best wishes.

The following Monday Alan delivered to me a sealed envelope written by his wife and addressed to me. 'Do you know what's in it Alan?'

'No, it's addressed to you.'

Alan's wife apologised to me and understood what a miserable afternoon we must all have endured. Inside I found the emergency ration. A couple of months later, Alan, looking extremely panicked, asked me for the emergency ration. Of course the reason was quickly established! Another emergency ration was quickly applied for.

While I worked with Alan I would make use of the lunch hour to do some training. Most of these occasions would be preceded by Alan asking me how old I was, which at this time was about 41.

'Ah, that is what we call "the cardiac *passage*". When I was a coroner's officer we had more people being brought in on the table between forty and fifty doing exercise than anything else. The cardiac *passage* . . . enjoy. By the way, if you're not back in an hour we'll get you collected.'

Thankfully I got through the cardiac *passage*.

Work cannot always be fun though, and policing has its moments of sadness. I was asked to return to my station one bright early Sunday morning to collect the details of a death message, which was too detailed to pass over the radio.

A steeplejack in his early forties had fallen from a high building he had been working on and needless to say he had died. I went to the address, not relishing having to share the news.

As I pulled up outside the address a woman came running across the road to me, she was full of the joys of spring. 'Can I help?' she asked.

'If I can come in please I don't like talking about other people's business on the street.' I have no doubt that as she opened her front door she knew what I was about to tell her, but obviously wanted to hear anything but.

As we got into her living room I saw a photograph of her recently deceased husband in a dinner jacket, with his arm around his wife. They had just celebrated their twenty-fifth wedding anniversary, and still appeared deeply in love, with many more happy years ahead of them. The photograph next to it was of their recently-born first grandchild. I was just about to destroy all of this harmony. It was horrible.

I had with me a young probationer, and immediately after I broke the news he got up to leave and the look I gave him made him sit straight back down. I spoke to a son-in-law on the telephone, apologised for breaking the news in such a terrible way and asked if he could inform his wife, the man's daughter.

After declining a cup of tea and thanking us for telling her the news we left her broken-hearted to get on with the rest of her life. I never found that this type of duty ever got any easier.

In the last year both my sons, also policemen, have recounted similar incidents to me of dealing with tragic incidents. I have seen them both in tears as they recounted incidents of having to deal with such a loss. One failed to save a young child despite doing CPR (cardiopulmonary resuscitation) and the other dealt with a fatal accident, later having to break the news to the family. It is days like this that make the funny episodes so special.

A little knowledge can be dangerous, most of us know that. A minicab pulled up outside the police station one morning, the driver complaining that his fare was refusing to pay his bill. The driver appeared reasonable and explained he had threatened to involve the police, but his passenger didn't care.

Our station sergeant went outside to investigate and established the full facts. There was no disagreement between the two parties as such – the passenger, who had been drinking, simply decided he didn't want to pay. Amazingly the grizzled old sergeant spent time trying to persuade the man to just pay the fare, but he wasn't having any of it. Finally the threat was made: 'If you don't pay the driver, I'll nick you.'

'Oh you will, will you. Just what power is that under?'

'That my friend is the Theft Act, just pay up and we can all get on our way, I'm very busy.'

'There isn't a power under the Theft Act. If you nick me I'll sue you.'

'You'll sue me, you'll sue me?'

'Yeah, I will, so put that in your pipe.'

With this the sergeant realised his powers of persuasion were not going to work that morning, so he confirmed the driver would supply a witness statement, which I was going to have to get, and promptly arrested our cab bilker. The reply to caution was something like, 'I'm going to sue your arse off. There isn't a power under the Theft Act. I know, I used to be in the job.'

'You must be referring to the 1968 Theft Act. Since you were at training school they introduced the 1978 Act, which you can look up after you get your charge sheet and the new Act deals with halfwits like you.'

The man was frogmarched in to the station, spluttering about 'What 1978 Theft Act?', but the sergeant was beyond talking at this point, his patience had been lost long since, along with the passenger of the cab's liberty.

I was posted at the front of Downing Street early one bright Sunday morning. This is usually a quiet duty, but Dave, who I was with, saw a couple walking towards us from Horseguards.

'Where do you think they are from?' he asked.

I looked at the bloke, who had bright chequered shorts, and his wife, not too dissimilar, and we both agreed that we thought they were probably American. This proved to be correct as the couple announced they were Betty and Bob from Ohio.

'We just think your Prime Minister Margaret Thatcher is just the greatest,' Bob declared.

'Thank you very much, that's very kind,' replied Dave.

'Yep, I was just saying to Betty, our President Ronald Reagan and her have a special relationship, ain't that right Betty?' She agreed with a nod of her head. Dave again thanked them and despite it being early in the day lifted the phone and asked to be put through to the Prime Minister.

'Did you hear that Betty, this officer is going to talk to the Prime Minister of the United Kingdom?' Bob looked awestruck and I looked as if I was going to break out giggling. I had to about turn as Dave continued, and he suddenly stood to attention.

'Good morning Prime Minister, it's Dave at the front of Downing Street here, I have Bob and Betty from Ohio here, they just wished to send their best wishes and say they think you are doing a fantastic job. Yes Prime Minister, I shall, thank you, goodbye.'

With this Bob from Ohio beamed at his wife and couldn't thank Dave enough as Dave informed them that Mrs T was very grateful. It was now time for me to go – I couldn't last much longer, the giggles were about to kick in. The dangerous mathematical formula had kicked in again. Boredom + policeman = mischief.

I have mentioned that I am a giggler, but I have worked with someone who is without doubt far worse than me. Terry and I had to visit another force to do a review on how they were doing things and report back as to whether the Met should follow suit.

We had to make our way to Cheshire so we booked a car out early in the morning and set off on our way. Needless to say we encountered one or two traffic problems, but to make the journey a little less boring we started to mimic the various accents of the relevant county we were in. At Birmingham I said in a very bad accent, 'Don't you think Terry that Birmingham has the most depressing accent in the entire country? Can you imagine waking up on a miserable day, looking out across Spaghetti Junction, turning on the radio and hearing the dulcet Birmingham tones, it must make you contemplate some terrible things.'

Terry as usual started giggling, he would be giggling before you barely started. This was only encouraging me, which makes me worse and as my wife says nothing will stop me now. As we got further north I broke out into the voice of a character from *Coronation Street* – the butcher who in the middle of a conversation would break out with, 'I say, I say' and then continue with his sentence. Terry was off again; he thought it was a good impersonation, I think he was on gas and air at this time. I also had to relay favourite scenes from some of our favourite shows, such as Corporal Jones in *Dad's Army*, or Tommy Cooper.

As we pulled in for a cup of tea and a break we were in the queue having a general chat when all of a sudden Terry walked off to a table, giggling and looking like a naughty boy. I quickly joined him with our tea when he said, 'You prat, you're still talking in that *Coronation Street* accent, you'll get us killed.' I honestly didn't realise. I was brought up to be polite, I certainly wouldn't have been intentionally offensive.

A couple of days later we met a large, recently retired detective chief inspector performing a civilian role in his force. As we sat down in his office he asked us how we were and in the middle of his sentence he said, 'I say, I say.' Terry did ever so well not breaking out in an attack of the giggles and an hour later we left, thanking the old detective for his help. Terry reminded me again that I was going to get us all killed, despite the fact, as I pointed out to him, that at that stage I had only said good morning. I got him into trouble one day with our boss, but the story is too non-PC to put on paper. I shall get complaints and I don't want any more of those.

A lot is made of community policing and rightly so. Home beats, as they used to be known, would spend a lot of time at various meetings with their local neighbourhood, including school visits.

A very busy home beat, whose beat covered an inner-city area, came back to the station after he had given a chat to a class of 9-year-olds. Bernie relayed the incident that had just taken place at one of his local schools. Whenever Bernie got angry or excited he would get a bit of a stammer and the story took some time telling as he kept breaking out in laughter, made worse with him stammering through the story.

Apparently the discussion had included what to do in an emergency and how to call for one of the emergency services. After explaining the need to remain calm Bernie explained the procedure. He also took along a telephone (no doubt today the entire class would have got their mobile phones out) and showed them what would happen when and if they used the 999 system. To make it light-hearted he decided they could all have a go and to make it more interesting they could make up any story they liked and Bernie would play the roll of the operator. The telephone was handed to one of the boys who correctly dialled the three nines.

'What emergency service do you require?' asked Bernie in an impersonation of a female operator.

'The police miss,' answered our 9-year-old, who was told he was being put through.

'You are through to the Information Room at Scotland Yard, what is the nature of your emergency?' Bernie was playing all the parts and using a large part of his repertoire of voices to keep the children interested.

'I've just seen some geezers wiv sawn-offs go into the bank,' the boy replied, very excited about delivering this news.

'What bank is this and where is it? Try to remain calm,' Bernie replied in a calming voice.

'It's the Nat West in the High Street.'

Bernie, not being able to lose the policemen in him, asked, 'Do you know any of the people with the shotguns?'

''Ere I may have told you there's a robbery going on, but I ain't no grass,' said the boy, and promptly slammed the phone down. It was sheer professionalism on Bernie's part that he managed to prevent himself from breaking out into laughter.

Just a couple of months before I retired I was posted to a night shift as duty officer. I set off with one of the local skippers who was going to drive me to my station so that I could collect all my personal protection equipment. I never did make it.

At our first attempt there was a call of a robbery, so off we went. I now realised I was a little out of touch because the modern police car is fitted with something called an MDT (mobile data terminal). Like everything else, these are simple to use, if you know how. I had completed a computer-based package to show me how to use an MDT, but I couldn't for the life of me remember. I didn't have a clue. While we were searching for the suspects, we found ourselves at the right location when the local authority CCTV team put up a suspect near to where we were. In moments we were on scene and yes, one arrest for robbery. This was good, I still enjoyed police work, and you can poke your MDT.

After completing some notes another call came out about youths breaking into a car. We drove near to the location, dropped our car off and jogged through to the scene of the call. As we got there three young men jumped into a car and accelerated away at high speed. I knew I was no longer the young lad of thirty years ago who was always chasing anything and everything, but I was off, it was like the old days. I knew this particular road was a cul-de-sac and I was sure there were no alleyways nearby. As I ran towards the car I was expecting to see some reverse lights coming on and find the car coming back towards me at a fast rate of knots. It didn't happen though, instead three doors were thrown open and all three occupants jumped out. I had always been taught to catch the driver. Passengers always deny they knew the car was stolen, but that is a little harder when you have been driving.

What good fortune! The two passengers were both about six feet tall and the driver about four-foot ten. My young, small, driver also followed fashion and long may it continue – as well as not being very tall, he had his trousers half way around his arse. I am told that if you don't do this you are not 'hip hop' and 'happening'. In my day you would have been called a delinquent.

Anyway, the driver decided he was going to make a run for it, did the worst job ever of trying to throw the keys away and then broke out into what he no doubt thought was a sprint. He attempted to sell me a dummy and run past me. I hadn't even moved. I was beginning to think this was a wind-up. As he picked up speed to something like three miles per hour I grabbed him by the collar and informed him his night had just got worse.

The other two were stopped and remained compliant as we established from our victims and witnesses that our three likely lads had stolen property from their car, which we quickly retrieved from theirs. After a long shift that I had thoroughly enjoyed I thought back to similar incidents and how fortunate I had been to have been part of them. I was still knackered though, old bones are old bones.

19

Interviews for Jobs Within the Job

In any job it is very likely that things will not always go the way you would like. This was no different for me. I had been moved at the end of my probation and this led to the commissioner of the day deciding that all uniform officers should be transferred once they had completed five years at their station. As this decision came out I had completed my five years service and having learned the area, its villains and another team, I was faced once again with another move.

One of my sergeants was just transferring to the Diplomatic Protection Group (DPG) and suggested that I apply for a position. It wasn't something that I wanted to do, but I didn't like the uncertainty of being posted to some of the stations available and I was now married and my eldest child had been born. I also needed to earn regular overtime if possible and this would definitely be available at the DPG.

Sure enough, a few weeks later the application came out in the weekly *Police Notices*. This document shows the details of every job vacancy in the Met, staff who were being promoted, officers being transferred, retiring or leaving. I had also been given my form to provide details of my preferred Divisions at this time and this made my mind up. I discussed it with my wife and she supported me in my decision – after all, I would be carrying a gun if the DPG accepted me and if I passed the subsequent firearms course.

I completed the necessary application and within a few weeks I was offered an interview, which was in the afternoon on my night duty week. The night before I did something I had never done before and volunteered to do station duty. This would ensure that I didn't finish late with a prisoner and I would also be able to prepare for the board, including amongst other things the Vienna Convention. This is an agreement between countries to provide the appropriate support for visiting diplomats. In the UK a number of embassies and foreign missions receive armed protection, which caused the formation of the DPG. Much of the work involved standing around and was far from the exciting life I had planned for myself – still, needs must.

My offer of station officer was quickly taken up and during the night I treated myself to a can of mulligatawny soup and a bar of chocolate, which broke up the studying nicely. About four hours or so later I had the most horrendous stomach pains and was having to navigate myself carefully between deciding what end I pointed at the loo. With little sleep I made my way to Central London, hoping that I would be able to make it through the interview. By 3.30 p.m., as I was waiting to be called in for my interview I was still breaking out into a sweat.

Eventually I was called in and saw that the chair was a superintendent, accompanied by two of his inspectors. After introducing myself I was invited to sit before the panel, which began to ask me questions, which I managed to answer without too many difficulties.

Finally the superintendent asked me what I would do if I returned home one day and my wife told me that she didn't want me to carry a gun any more. So I explained that we had discussed this in detail and she was fully aware of all the dangers, but she was comfortable with the fact that I may have to use a gun and I could possibly face the eventuality where I might be fired at.

'No, no, no, no, I don't mean *now*, I'm talking about several months from now, if we were to make the mistake of accepting you to the DPG.'

I was now beginning to have another attack of the sweats and the messages from my stomach were not feeling positive either.

Couldn't they just bring this to an end, I'd been in the damn room for over twenty minutes by now.

'Well sir, if I went home and my wife told me that she didn't want me to carry a gun any longer, the next day that I was at work I would give you a 728 requesting that I be returned to normal duty.'

'So you're telling me lad that you would give in to your wife, just like that?' demanded the superintendent.

'Oh yes sir, let's be honest about this, my wife is far more important to me than you ever will be.' Please finish this I thought, just send me packing, I know I need the overtime but I really didn't want a terrible accident in front of these three senior officers. All went quiet and one of the inspectors covered his face with his hands.

'OK,' said the superintendent, 'I don't have any further questions.' And he confirmed this with his inspectors, so I was released, and immediately had only one place to go.

After I came out of the toilet I bumped into one of the inspectors from the board, who told me that I would be getting one of the vacancies. He continued, 'By the way, the superintendent commented that he had never been spoken to like that before, he was impressed with your strength of character and honesty.' I was amazed. I thought I had blown it.

The trip back home on the train was not quite as bad as I was expecting, but there were still further visits to the loo, I am happy to say when I got indoors and not before. My team were further amazed when I offered to do yet another posting in the station office. Needs must.

Some years later I had to report sick with an even worse bout of food poisoning than the one I described above. In between visits to the toilet I wrote an email to a mate of mine who at the time was posted to Bosnia.

I have just had to report sick for the first time in several years, I have got mathematical disease ... I'm going to the loo every thirty minutes and the train journey to London alone is over forty, do you think I have made the right decision?

Many years later I was on another interview board. On this occasion I was attempting promotion and the interview was the final stage to decide whether I would be suitable or not. As I entered the room I was faced with only two people, one of whom pointed out immediately that there was water available if I wished to make use of it. I thought I had better prepare myself at the start rather than in mid-flow, if you'll forgive the pun, so I began to pour the water into the paper cup. As I did this I was asked a question and as I looked up I knocked the cup over leaving a nice pool of water on the table. What a plonker, I should have held the cup properly.

'Sorry about that, I normally do that to try and settle myself down at times like this.' I fully expected both of them to laugh at my expense, but I was more unsettled when neither of them did. I was certainly up against a couple of old pros here.

After I left the interview I bumped into another colleague who had just gone through the same experience. I was being ultra critical of myself as I tend to do in these situations and it was made worse when he explained how well his interview had gone. He explained that he had done this, followed up by some of that, and they couldn't possibly be anything other than impressed. Oh great, I didn't do anything at all like that, which made me feel even more fed up. Amazingly, when the results came out I had passed and my colleague had failed. You just can never tell.

One of the teams I worked on was full of Scottish officers. I have mentioned before that when you work with others you do attune to their accents. We had a vacancy for someone to work in the control room so Jim, one member of the 'Jock Squad' as they were known (pre-PC days) spoke to our inspector, who was known as a 'Posh Jock'. He didn't have your usual Scottish accent and had been schooled at a nice school somewhere else. 'Sir, sir,' Jim called. 'I've just seen there is a vacancy for the control room, I'd be interested.'

'Don't' waste your time Jim, I was brought up in Scotland and when you are on the radio even I don't know what the f**k you're saying. Application denied.' This may not be very politically correct, but it saved a lot of writing.

With no further ado Jim thanked the boss for considering it and went about his duties, like the good soldier he was.

20

Senior Officers and Line Managers

In my early months on Division JD, who was the Federation representative, was recounting one of his recent meetings with the chief superintendent. The police cannot strike, so instead of a union we have a Federation which represents officers below the rank of superintendent on discipline, pay and conditions. At each of the stations you have representatives who can approach the bosses on a variety of issues.

This particular occasion had been just before the run-up to Christmas. The duties had been published and at each station the number of patrolling vehicles had been halved in an attempt to save money. At this particular time budgets were far more lax than they are today. Due to the poor pay in the 70s a lot of the team were happy to work Christmas because you were paid double time. Their mindset had not changed despite the fact that the government of the day had just given us a massive rise to halt the number of officers that were leaving as they could no longer afford to stay.

Armed with the Christmas rotas JD made an appointment to see the boss who clearly understood what the conversation was to be about. As JD entered the office the boss called out, 'It's no good you asking me to rescind my order on the number of vehicles out on the Bank Holidays JD, so you may as well save yourself the bother.' JD was always very good in these situations and was somehow able to provide this cherubic look on his face as if butter wouldn't melt, despite the fact that the boss knew only too well that this wasn't the case.

'Oh sir, how could you think such a thing? As the Federation rep I understand totally that you have to do what you think is right. Oh no, I am here in the interests of my members of course, all year round they are refused time off, because their stations fall below the minimum number of vehicles that are required to be posted. Now we all follow orders, all I would ask is that you formalise this with a written instruction to your supervisors that as of now such requests will not be denied providing there is one vehicle available at each station, is that not reasonable sir?'

'Bugger off JD, you conniving old sod, and you can tell "your members" that I shall increase the number of cars back to normal for the Bank Holidays.'

JD concluded his tale that another successful meeting on behalf of his members had been agreed by the ever hard-working representative, who only ever had their interests at heart and there would be more officers now available to work for 'double bubble' (this was the common saying by officers when they were working on a Bank Holiday).

I have been fortunate to work for some great bosses, but of course you will undoubtedly meet some that by choice you would rather have avoided. When I first went to the DPG, I didn't have two coins to rub together. We had bought our home a year earlier, the mortgage rate had gone through the roof, my wife was on maternity leave and she didn't want to go back to work, and I was happy about that.

I had been at the DPG a few months when I was asked by one of the sergeants if I was going out for a drink with the team. I had already told someone else on the team that I couldn't, but he pushed the point and eventually I admitted that I didn't have the funds and felt somewhat belittled as a couple of other members of the team sat around listening in. I wasn't enjoying myself at this time, I missed general police duties, but the overtime was beginning to help us. With this the skipper informed me that he would be going to work at Headquarters soon and as I was still in my probationary period (which was six months) I could find myself going back to Division.

I have never taken kindly to being threatened. One of the reasons I joined the job was to go and help others in similar situations. Bullies for me have a number of personal problems that they can't talk to others about, or are too afraid to face. This invariably causes them to take it out on others, but I wasn't about to become an 'other'.

I put my face rather close to his and said, 'I couldn't give a f**ck and furthermore I have been threatened by people who actually scare me and you're not even on the fu**ing list.' I was totally out of order in the manner I chose to deal with this moron, but followed it up to the few idling around. 'If any of you don't like that we can always discuss the matter elsewhere.'

There was deadly silence, when the sergeant finally recovered from the shock and said, 'I suppose you are going to join the knitting brigade on this team.' With that one of the guys entered the room and asked me if I wanted a game of darts before we had to go out to our next duty, which I accepted, looking at the sergeant and saying, 'If you don't mind Sarge I'm going to knit one, pearl one.' I didn't find myself back to normal duties in the immediate future, but occasionally you have to stand up to be counted. I'm glad that I did. A more professional approach would probably have been much better though.

Some years later I was a sergeant myself and we had just finished our monthly training day. The conclusion of the day was for some poor member of the senior management team to field any questions we had. On this occasion our superintendent did the honours. He wasn't a bad bloke, there was no malice in him as far as I was aware. His nickname was Boycie, due to his similar appearance of the well known character in *Only Fools and Horses*.

I was with Len, who by now had completed his thirty years' service and we were idling and gossiping in the station yard. As we did this the superintendent came along and Len, who didn't get on with this senior officer, enquired what he and his family were going to be doing at the coming Christmas, only four or five weeks away. Quite rightly you could see suspicion enter the super's face, but believing it was part of the Christmas spirit he relaxed and began to go into detail about the festive occasion on Christmas day at one family, followed by events for the Boxing Day with the other part of his family. All of this would culminate in a joint event on New Year's Eve.

'Oh that is very nice for you all,' Len said, and gave an inviting smile towards the superintendent, whose defences were most definitely down at this time. Not only did he feel obliged to ask, but he actually seemed to want to enquire what Len and his family had planned for the Festive Season.

'Well sir, unfortunately this year the twenty-fifth and twenty-sixth of December have completely caught the duties office off guard, with them not realising those are the days regularly known to the rest of us as Christmas Day and Boxing Day. Nobody has been able to work out what the hell is going on and furthermore we can't find out, despite various visits to the duties office, whether we shall be working or not. So I have made it very easy for them. I have informed them that under no circumstances will I be driving the area car this Christmas. I shall follow your example and spend it with my family at home. Have a good one sir.'

With this Len walked off, with the poor superintendent looking somewhat flabbergasted, calling, 'You will have to wait and see Len.'

We had other nicknames for the management at this station at the time. The chief superintendent bore a remarkable resemblance to the original Milky Bar Kid and the personnel manager was called 'Pizza Face', due to an acne complaint. I can sympathise there, although he and I didn't see eye to eye on certain things. In fact it was another training day when the personnel manager announced that his unit would no longer be sending out appraisals to officers to complete, the line managers would have to attend the office and collect them.

I said that I couldn't see what benefit that had for the supervisors, as half the shifts they worked and more were when his unit was closed. Despite this he was adamant that this was the way forward and besides it would be good development for the sergeants.

I informed him that I was certain that the rest of the sergeants all knew the way to the station, it was the same route to take prisoners and I certainly didn't think that such a development would take much achieving. I asked if his unit could send the reports out at the beginning of every month to each team inspector. In turn the inspectors could ensure that they were returned at the end of that month and at the same time monitor their sergeants, and ensure they were completing them on time, and comment when their appraisals were due.

'Absolutely not, I have made my mind up,' Pizza Face declared.

I appealed to the superintendent but he didn't find me appealing either and despite the fact I thought such units were there to support the police officers I announced that as a service it was at best 'rubbish'. The matter was brought to an abrupt end when the superintendent told me it was. You can't win them all.

Pizza Face was also politically correct to the point of ridiculousness. My inspector at the time had requested more female officers, when he was jumped on by Mr PC. 'Inspector, we live in a world of equal opportunities now, don't you mean "constable"?'

'No, I don't mean that at all. I have one female officer on my team and unless we change the Police and Criminal Evidence Act searches should be carried out by officers of the same sex as the prisoner, unless you wish to defend the MPS when we are being sued because some female prisoner has been searched by one of the blokes.' A deathly hush ensued for a short period before it was agreed that the request did after all make sense.

The management came to find out about their nicknames in an unfortunate incident, where one officer was suspected of acting inappropriately and in order to identify the culprit the telephones were being monitored. During the investigation the conversations of a number of officers were listened to, but what amazed me was the fact they managed to identify the culprit as they intended to, but they couldn't work out who Pizza Face was. There you go.

After the Milky Bar Kid moved on we of course had a new boss. He was a reasonable bloke, although I didn't agree with his idea of keeping me in custody for a year, but there you are.

I used to cycle to work a lot of the time at this stage and one early morning before I changed into my uniform I dropped into the office I was working in, still dressed in my cycling outfit. As I approached the boss saw me. I wasn't expecting him in for a couple of hours. He looked at my cycling top, which bore the head of a ram. 'Ah, are you an Aries?' he asked.

'No sir, my wife bought it for me, do you think she is trying to tell me something?'

He wasn't too impressed with this and walked off mumbling something that I couldn't make out. I found out later that he was a religious man and I didn't mean to offend him. For the benefit of the reader, I bought the top in a sale, as simple as that. Any other thoughts are just ideas of grandeur on my part.

One of my earliest negative encounters with a senior officer followed my transfer to a new station after completing my probation. As I have mentioned, I didn't want to go. I was at a fantastic station, which was nice and busy, yet I was going to be moved to a quieter one. On day one I attended in plenty of time and waited until I was finally called in to the boss's office.

I had been directed that I should stand to attention about three feet from the desk and wait to be addressed. I followed the instructions of the kind lady and waited until eventually the senior officer, who was deeply engrossed in some paperwork, acknowledged my existence. Without looking up he asked me what I thought of the commander's idea of moving all probationers at the end of their probationary period of two years. I didn't want to get off to the wrong start and I was certainly not going to say that in my case it was a negative step, so I told him that the commander was in charge and I respected that. There were four stations that the chief superintendent could send me to, and out of the four there was one which I really wanted, one which I really didn't and the other two I could cope with.

He announced that he would send me to my first choice. Oh thank you, dear God. I also thanked the boss who now looked up and noticed that I was pleased with his choice. Clearly this would not do so he said, 'On second thoughts I shall send you to . . .' wait for it, no please, not my last choice, please. Fortunately it wasn't as he gave me one of the other two.

I could see he was pleased with himself and I later discovered that he was a most disagreeable person, universally disliked by all the teams, which continued throughout the eighteen months that he remained in charge. As I looked at him I thought, the last thing I am going to do is give you the pleasure of seeing that you have bested me, so I calmly said, 'Thank you very much sir, that is very kind, it is even nearer to my home and will mean even less travelling.' Put that in your pipe and let it choke you, I thought. With this I had clearly taken up far too much of his time so he returned his attention to his paperwork. He allowed me to stand to attention though for another two minutes or so before he dismissed me. Oh dear, oh dear. Still, you can't win them all.

I managed to upset the above senior officer unintentionally one day. I had been posted to the control room and he had a good idea. On a wall was a list, amongst other things of home beats, who would book on with the control room, so that we would know they were on duty. It was a good idea. This happened as I sat waiting for another telephone call one early shift when one of the home beats announced that he was covering the property office. As the box was quite small I managed to write 'PROP OFF' with the thick marker pen.

Having exhausted myself I went for my breakfast, which was just as well. Whilst I was keeping man and soul together the chief superintendent visited the control room to declare he had no idea what PROP OFF meant. My colleague was quick to announce that I was responsible and the duty inspector was called. Upon my return the duty officer was waiting. He clarified that I had been responsible for this heinous outrage and informed me that the chief super had not been able to work it out. Consequently I was now banned from the control room (result) and I had to be thrown out of the station to the farthest beat in order that I would learn the error of my ways.

'I understand completely sir, sorry I have let you down. Can I just have the order written in my pocket book in case another supervisor wants me in here in the future, I would like to have it all officially recorded.'

I believe the smile on my face may have been the wrong response, so I had to leave the station and leave very quickly as I had now upset my duty officer.

Some years ago I was told by a long-serving officer that I should never try to understand the mind of senior officers, it was like trying to make sense of the universe. It would be a dark place that I may regret visiting. He supported this with a query that had been raised when he had been at Erith police station.

A senior officer from a department at Scotland Yard had telephoned the station office, confirmed he was through to the right location and promptly explained his call.

'I have been thinking about the Greenwich Barrier. In the event of it being used in a high water situation it would get awfully wet down your end.'

'That is quite correct,' the station officer confirmed.

'Well I've been thinking your location would be ideal for a Thames River Police unit to be stationed, what do you think of that?'

'Well sir, I admire your way of thinking. I totally agree, perhaps you could have a word with another senior officer who moved them about a year ago, having been stationed here for over a hundred years.'

'Oh.'

I do recall a story and I never did clarify the authenticity of it, but it's a good story nonetheless, which happened some years ago at New Scotland Yard. Apparently the incident occurred one afternoon when an inspector for one reason or another had decided to visit a local pub. This wouldn't have been a problem, except he was still on duty and had more than a couple. Officers cannot drink on duty except for certain occasions and when they are authorised.

Our slightly inebriated inspector decided to return to work. As you enter the foyer of New Scotland Yard you can enter the actual building through a revolving door. As our drinker entered one side to gain entry a very senior officer entered the other side in order to leave. At moments like this perhaps a wild imaginative story came to his mind about a 'what would you do if . . . ?'

Well our friend thought it would be a very good idea to spin the senior officer around in the revolving door, which he did and continued to do in between shouts from the senior officer to get someone to stop him. When this could finally be achieved our inspector, through a couple of drinks and dizziness, fell out in something of a heap. This foolish act very quickly resulted in him being moved from his specialist department back to regular duties.

When the inspector arrived at his new station, he met his new chief superintendent who told him that he would be keeping a very close eye on him. The inspector said that since the incident things had become difficult at home and the chief super should not be too surprised if he was thrown out, resulting in him bunking down somewhere in the station. With this the chief superintendent had heard enough, and told him to sort himself out and get on with it.

A few weeks later one Monday morning as the chief superintendent arrived at his office he found the inspector cooking a fry-up on a campus stove immediately outside his office. 'Good morning sir,' he greeted his boss, 'I'm just about to fry some eggs, how do you like yours done?' The chief shouted that he couldn't be doing with this and directed that somebody sort him out, he was beyond help. Shortly after that our inspector took early retirement.

I have worked for some very good bosses. I even had one that became my supplier. He was the one who introduced me to cappuccinos. At first he started me with one a day, but before long it became two, then two at each visit to our local dealer. Before long it had control of me, I needed a regular fix. He was a very nice guy and he explained to me and one of our other regular coffee mates, Terry (giggler) that he had always wanted an Audi A4 and when he retired some months later he was going to treat himself.

On the night of his retirement do we had compiled a 'this is you life' book for him, which the chief superintendent used as part of his leaving speech. Inside on a sheet of A4 I printed a car with the words, 'this isn't my only A4 you know'. After he left I gradually began to get my life back under control as I dealt with my caffeine addiction, sort of.

Of course as individuals senior officers have their own style of operating. A few years before I retired the crime reporting system we were using needed to be upgraded. I received an email from my chief inspector telling me and the other team inspectors that ALL officers had to complete the new training in order to be able to cope with the new system. The new procedures were neatly captured in an eighty-page document.

The memo further stated that there should only be one copy per team and no time would be given to allow for this training off-team, but all teams would complete this by the deadline set and this was for strict compliance. This is one thing that really winds me up. Strict compliance. The police service is a disciplined job, if you are given a lawful order you get on with it, moan if you want, I certainly have done, but you get on with it. As for one copy that was ridiculous so I printed up a copy for each of my sergeants and directed them to ensure that each of their respective officers completed the training as per the boss's directions.

I replied to the chief inspector while I still had the hump, not normally a good idea I know. 'Sir, I shall ensure that all the officers on my team will complete the training as per your directions. I

174

note the document is only eighty pages in length, perhaps if someone could email me the *Encyclopaedia Britannica* I shall get on with that next week.' I didn't get a bollocking or even a reply, someone had to be grown up after all.

A couple of years ago we got a new very senior officer at our station. She had been meeting with the heads of all the various departments and I got a call for my boss to go and meet her. Unfortunately he was on leave, which resulted in me giving her an update on what the team did.

First impressions are important and I liked this senior officer, despite the fact that she informed me that if officers messed up she collected their genitalia. I informed her that if our team did mess up it would certainly not be intentional and besides, I added using a Forrest Gump-type voice, I didn't want to become jewellery and I was certain my boss didn't either. She laughed at this and I thought 'thank Christ for that, someone with some balls and a sense of humour, all is not lost'.

21

Other Training on the Job

Despite leaving training school and completing your probationer training over the course of two years there was always other training. I mentioned that my bandaging techniques were not very good, but when I started you had to do first aid refresher training, simply known as FART. This had to be done every three years until you had twenty-two years' service, when it was deemed that you should have sufficient understanding of the subject. Today you have to do an annual refresher test until you retire, which is far better, particularly for someone like me who is not naturally gifted in this area. A few months ago when I did my last refresher we were shown how to use the CPR machine – what a fantastic bit of kit. The job certainly was improving in many ways.

At my first FART in the job it was my last two days before my long weekend and the start of a night duty. Let's face it, after three years you deserve a FART. I thought I was an old lag in the job now, so I thought I would forgo a shave only to find one of my old inspectors from my previous station also doing his refresher. I was immediately questioned as to why I had chosen not to shave. I informed him of my shift pattern and said, 'Well sir as you know the instruction book states that when an officer is considering growing any facial hair they should consider doing so when they are on annual leave, night duty or when they are performing duty away from the public.' I hadn't used this two years earlier and I knew the wording better this time. The inspector looked at me in an attempt to get me to change my mind, but I didn't. So he simply said, 'We both know that's a load of bo**ocks.'

'Actually sir, only one of us knows for definite, the other person only thinks they do.' Oh, just when I thought I wasn't going to have a good FART. Bomber would have been proud of me. At the end of the two days we were questioned by a doctor on a number of points we had learned. I thought I had failed, but I did manage to do the resuscitation as taught and I think it was that alone that got me through. My bandages had barely improved and I didn't recognise the symptoms for heat stroke or hypothermia.

At about the end of the 70s the Met trained officers in shield use. I found the instructors were way over the top at this time, getting very excited about quite often silly little things, or so they seemed to me. They would always be shouting and I don't think this intimidated a lot of coppers, in fact I think it wound a lot of them up.

One of the old sweats was told he had to sprint from the starting point to a line about fifteen yards away (if you are young a yard is about 7.5 centimetres less than a metre), sprint back to the start, return to another line twenty five yards away, return again to the starting line before making the final sprint to a line some forty yards away and back.

We were lined up into three teams and the instructor explained that this was a competition. Those who came last would receive a punishment. With this the whistle was blown and two of the teams were off like long dogs. Dave, who started for the other team, trotted off very gently, very gently indeed. This wasn't good enough, so he was faced with a lot of shouting, which just made him go slower until the instructor demanded he go faster, whereupon Dave came to a complete stop and told him to stop shouting as he was getting a headache.

'I told you to go faster.'

Dave simply replied, 'If I told you to go f**k yourself you might do it. I on the other hand have absolutely no intention of going at any speed other than the one I choose.'

With this the instructor decided to tell him to go back to his station. Dave accepted this, informing the instructor that he already was at his station, but was happy not to have to do shield training again. Strangely enough though the overweight PC quickly became a running enthusiast soon after this event and lost a few stones in weight. Perhaps some of the shouting had got through after all.

We had to do our shield refresher training every six months then, and on one such trip out I found this aggressive little squat instructor calling me and one of the other guys out to do a practical. We were informed that we had received a call that a man was armed with a knife and pointed to the location we could find him, a specially prepared room. We had two minutes to prepare before taking any appropriate action. I had seen this instructor in action before, one of our decent inspectors asked him a reasonable question one day and boy did he get excited.

As I discussed our course of action with John I asked him if he had had any dealings with the instructor, which he had, but he had not witnessed anything like I had. I told John that this little s**it was going to do his best to make us look stupid. We had to keep our shields locked together until we could herd the instructor in to a corner of the room and then pin him up against a wall, as we had been shown.

As we entered the room with our shields locked together we could see the instructor was holding a plastic training knife and he began to circle us, trying to make us react and cause our shields to break apart. But John and I kept following him and gradually we corralled him in to the corner. Without a word from either of us we both rammed him against the wall together, it must have been a little uncomfortable for him to say the least. With this he shouted, 'OK, OK, you've won.' I simply told him to drop the knife or else (I had discovered my own 'or else' at this point). He refused, saying, 'It's all over, just let me go.' So I jammed my shield on the top of his steel toecap boot and told him if he didn't drop it the next one would be in the shin. He got the idea and finally conceded defeat.

*

179

I have played a number of sports over the years and I would have thought that would have given me reasonable abilities of coordination. Not the case at all, I am rubbish. When we were all first issued with our own handcuffs we were also reminded of some of the arrest restraints we had been taught at Hendon. The job has got a lot better, with officers doing officer safety training, which they are required to do a couple of times a year, going over the correct use of the asp or baton, handcuffs and spray as well as good use of restraints.

At shield training one day we had another over-enthusiastic instructor who quickly identified my lack of coordination. Shouting, always the damn shouting, does it make a point any clearer I ask you, by shouting? I was questioned as to whether I practised the techniques during my grub breaks.

'No I don't.'

More shouting with, 'Well you should practise during your grub break, that way you wouldn't be so crap.'

I had to agree it was a fair point; I was crap, so I asked, 'Do you take a panda out during your grub break and remind yourself how to make an arrest?'

'Why the f**k should I do that?' the large instructor asked.

'Well, if we are all going to practise all the policing skills we might need, you might want to give it some thought so you don't get too rusty.'

With this he told me that I didn't have to do shield training. *What?* I actually didn't realise this at the time and despite doing all my refresher training and then some, I was rarely used on shield aid anyway.

'Oh I didn't realise that, can I go now?'

Apparently I couldn't, but I didn't go back, I moved on to another job, which didn't require me to be shield trained any more. Oh dear.

*

When I became a firearms officer, just after they replaced the flintlock and powder muskets, we had to be tested every four months on the Smith & Wesson .38, a six-round revolver, which was the weapon of choice for the police at this time.

On this refresher I met up with one of the sergeants on my team when I had been a probationer. He was now with CO19 as it was known. We had a little chat and then we got down to the nuts and bolts of the day.

After loading our guns with six rounds, we put another six rounds in a speed strip to use as and when directed. On this shoot my old skipper Brian decided to make it more interesting. We would face our targets, fire two shots and return to our normal positions. This would be repeated and at that point we would take the opportunity to reload the four spent cartridges. After firing another four rounds we would reload with another two and all the remaining rounds would then be used as the target turned to face us. This should total us using twelve rounds and scoring a possible twenty-four points. If this makes sense, congratulations, because I didn't have my thinking head on that day and I hadn't been paying close enough attention. I had my Wurzel day-dreamer's head on. It was a better fit.

Of course I found I was pulling the trigger and I suppose you could say I was firing blanks, certainly nothing was happening and at this point I realised that I had messed it up. Rather than admit this I fired the other rounds as soon as I could, but of course I was captured. After being told that I still had mush between my ears Brian pointed out to the rest of the class the dangers I had highlighted. He was right of course. Let's face it, this is a serious business, there can't be any room for complacency.

Another good addition to the police force was the 'enforcer'. This is a short but very heavy metal ram that is used for opening doors to make a speedy entry. When we first got these officers were being sent on a course to use them. I didn't think there was too much to it, I never did do the course, but to be fair the job has to protect itself for good reason.

I was running an estates team at the time and we had a drugs warrant to execute. Someone suggested that we use the enforcer, although we didn't have anyone who was trained, but we took it with us anyway. We had already worked out how we were going to execute the small operation, except who was going to use the enforcer. As I was meant to be in charge I thought I should lead from the front. If you have seen the television programmes you will know that you need to make a speedy entry, take control of the area and conduct a thorough and methodical search – this increases the chances of success and reduces the chance of injury to the officers and those inside the house.

As I got to the relevant door (there are stories of the wrong doors being attacked) I gained some momentum with the heavy weight before delivering a decent blow against the lock. It was at this time that I discovered that only the Yale lock was on and the door flew open. As I entered, which I hadn't intended (training would have helped here) I ran past a large Rottweiler sitting just inside the door. 'Oh s**t,' went through my mind, because this had not been mentioned in the intelligence-gathering, or the observations. I didn't fancy running past the dog as I would have been trapped at the end of the hall so I ran up the stairs leaving the dog behind, which was looking totally bewildered. Fortunately he turned out to be a good dog, unlike most dogs in drug houses.

I have had a few run-ins with dogs over the years. A couple of the guys on one of my teams both wanted to join the Dog Section at about the same time the Dangerous Dogs Act came into force, so they began to do everything in their power to rid our area of any illegal pit bulls. As the sergeant I had to go along whenever the warrants were executed, which must have been about forty in total.

At one address the warrant was nearing its expiry (you only get up to a calendar month to execute it), so we decided to get the dog that was running loose despite the owner still not showing up at the address. We had the assistance of the Dog Section and a cunning plan. Quite simply the cunning plan didn't work (Black-adder and Baldrick would have been proud) and at one point the dog was running loose around the house, his house, which we were in and which we hadn't been invited into.

My youngest son at this time loved Spiderman so I would watch the cartoons with him. As the dog came towards me looking very nervous and very underfed I attempted a reverse Spiderman, which as you probably know, is walking backwards up a wall. Unsurprisingly it didn't work. I could have messed myself, but fortunately someone up there was looking after me, not for the first or the last time I might add, and the dog ran away, before the Dog Unit finally managed to get the damn dog catchers on it and allow us to take it away. No, this time the dog wasn't going in the back of a van with me either.

When I returned to my station after completing a course for sergeants I explained how painful it had been. We had definitely hit a 'pink and fluffy' stage, accompanied with beanbags. It wasn't my cup of tea, but I grinned and bore it. A fellow skipper thanked me for letting him know, he was going back to the training school for the same course in a few weeks, and he was really looking forward to it. I had made his day. When he went back for his course he managed to get about halfway through the first week when the instructor asked him if he was all right.

'No not really, I've never heard so much nonsense as I have this week. I could be learning about any number of useful things, but what do we get? How to deal with appraisals and that took us half a day to cover. That could have been covered in an hour at the most. From what I have been told by others that have been subjected to this course that is about the highlight, it goes down from here.'

'If you don't like this course you can go back to your station.'

'Thank you very much I will, it's probably the only thing that you and I are ever going to agree on.'

'You'll have to go and see our chief inspector before you leave and tell him your thoughts.'

'Oh don't worry about him, I'll go and see whoever the most senior person is here and we can cut out the middle man.'

With this they went off to the senior officer's room where a full and frank discussion was had, resulting in John returning to his station, and he later presented himself to his own chief inspector.

'I've just been on the phone to the training school chief inspector, he tells me you think their course is crap, what on earth do you think you are doing?'

'Well sir, the chief inspector is quite correct. The course is crap and rather than have a cushy couple of weeks doing nine to five I would rather do late turn or night duty for the rest of the time if it means I don't have to go back to that place.'

I had to admire his strength of character, I only thought it was crap, I certainly didn't say it to the boss.

I am pleased to say that these courses, having gone through the pink and fluffy stage, resorted to a more sensible approach soon after this.

A lot of training is now done on a computer, and it is painful. One day there was a particularly horrible piece of training that everyone had to do. One of the sergeants clarified with Tony that he wasn't busy, which was handy as Tony was very good with computers.

'Ah that's very useful, I'm going to give you a choice. You can go out immediately and get wet, or you can complete this bloody training for me, which must be done today or I'm dead meat, what would you prefer?'

'I think I would like to do your training for you sergeant.'

About thirty minutes later Tony declared he had finished the training.

'Excellent Tony what score did I get?' the sergeant asked.

'You got one hundred per cent sarge.'

'Quite right as well Tony, I couldn't possibly set a bad example to the rest of the team could I? Let's hope everyone else is as diligent as us. Was that the kettle I heard just going on?'

22

All Good Things Must Come to an End

About a month before I retired my wife and I went on holiday for two weeks on a Mediterranean cruise. We had celebrated our silver wedding anniversary a few months earlier and we had decided to spoil ourselves. Our children were grown up and we were in our fifties, so why not. I had already submitted my retirement papers and I now had the chance to think about whether I was doing the right thing or not. I just had to go back to work for a few weeks before hanging up my warrant card and starting a new chapter in my life.

When I returned to work I managed to tidy up most of the things that I wanted to and hand over to my successor. I really thought at one time of just walking away without even having a leaving drink, but again my wife said I shouldn't do that.

I didn't have a big fancy do, which some people choose to. I just wanted to have a few drinks with those I had worked with over the last couple of years and quietly move on. I didn't have any regrets, although you do miss your colleagues and the day-to-day banter.

There are a couple of people I would ignore if I saw them in the street tomorrow, you can probably guess from the book who they might be, but in thirty years that's not bad really, there are hundreds of others I would stop to talk to and find out how they are and how things were going in the job. Of course I still have a pint with some of my ex-colleagues and we enjoy swinging the lamp as we talk about the good old days.

I thought of some of the good times and some of the less good ones. The occasions you have to go and tell a loved one that their partner isn't coming home. Seeing a smiling face after you have helped someone through a difficult situation always made my day. It all makes the job worthwhile.

No I couldn't be maudlin, I had been fortunate to have enjoyed my thirty years of police service. It had been a great job.

X Badly written 5/7